WHERE THE RIVERS FLOW

WHERE THE RIVERS FLOW

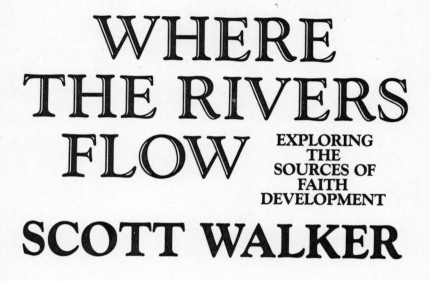

EXPLORING
THE
SOURCES OF
FAITH
DEVELOPMENT

SCOTT WALKER

WORD BOOKS
PUBLISHER
WACO, TEXAS

A DIVISION OF
WORD, INCORPORATED

To the past . . .
  my father, Al Walker

And to the future . . .
  my sons, Drew and Luke

Contents

CONTENTS

II. WHERE THE RIVERS FLOW

Foreword

In this book, Scott Walker has recorded the spiritual pilgrimage of a child "born into" a faith in a Christian fellowship that does not believe in infant baptism. But whereas he was not immersed in the waters of baptism, he was indeed immersed in the life of the church, the fellowship of believers, as he grew from birth to maturity.

He tells this story, which puts into words the struggle of the souls of many children, adolescents, and young adults who "cut their teeth" on church pews. He has given us here an "interior" view of a child's concrete thinking about a "Santa-Claus-like" world. The severe trauma of an early adolescent losing his father suddenly in death by a heart attack thrusts him into extended wrestlings of an adolescent mind with doubt, the hunger for certainty, and the need for a clear sense of God's calling in his life.

As a pastor and a father now, with the great decisions of early maturity behind him, he devotes the second section of the book to his own confession of faith, which he believes quite rightly will serve as a guide for you and me in our appropriation of the faith of our fathers as we work out our own spiritual world view.

I commend this book to your reading. It is a living human document on "coming of age" as a Christian.

WAYNE E. OATES, PH.D.

Professor of Psychiatry and Behavioral Sciences
Director, Program in Ethics and Pastoral Counseling
University of Louisville School of Medicine

Acknowledgments

If we lived in a truly just world, an author's name would seldom appear alone on the cover of a book. Rather, beside the writer's name would also be printed the names of those who contributed significantly to the composition of the manuscript. For in truth, writing is a joint labor of love, combining the talents of many people.

In this spirit, I would like to thank Lottie Baucum for her painstaking critique and correction of the rough draft of my manuscript. Within the span of a few weeks, she taught me more about English grammar than years of formal education were able to impart.

I am also greatly indebted to the editorial skills of Anne Christian Buchanan of Word Books. A true professional, she often took "muddy river water" and made it crystal clear. I also found Anne to be a source of patience and encouragement, a blessed characteristic when working with opinionated authors.

As I come to write these closing lines before publication, I am keenly aware that without the support and sponsorship of Floyd Thatcher there would be no publication. I will always be thankful to Floyd for his encouragement, his advice, and his being "a friend at the door." Floyd is that rare person who enables others to create.

Finally, a word of loving thanks to my wife, Beth, who never tired of reading chapter revisions. Without her love, understanding, and gentle nature, this story would never have been told.

SCOTT WALKER

To the Reader

Books are not simply written. Like a human baby, they are conceived within the life of an individual, carried for a long period of time, and finally thrust into the world because there is no other choice but to give birth—to write. For a long time, I have had incubating within me some thoughts about the evolution of Christian faith, thoughts which I feel a need to express to others. Trying to give birth to these thoughts by verbalizing them has indeed caused some labor pains. But the process has been truly worthwhile for me.

I have chosen to write this book, however, not only from my own urge to communicate but also out of a desire to help others who are struggling to develop Christian faith. As a pastor, I often find myself in a position to share life with people who are truly searching for a faith that has integrity. In today's world, faith in anything is something not easily achieved. Faith in God can sometimes seem all but impossible. I have written to help those who honestly seek to understand better how faith in God and a relationship with Christ are actualized. If God can shed some light upon your path through my lantern, then praise be to him.

In technical terms, this book is about "faith development." In other words, it seeks to isolate and delineate those aspects of life that contribute to the development of religious faith, in general, and Christian faith, in particular. But let me hasten to say that this is not a technical book.

I believe the development of faith is a subject that should be approached in a very personal manner, because the evolution of faith is always an intimate process. An overly empirical or analytical approach to understanding faith often distorts—perhaps even slanders—the very subject of faith being studied. Consequently, as I have grappled with how to communicate my thoughts most clearly, I have been drawn again and again to the autobiographical form of writing. As a doctoral student at the University of Georgia studying in the area of adult development, I was repeatedly impressed by the fact that the greatest truths in life are often best communicated biographically or autobiographically—in story form—rather than through analysis or exposition.

Jesus must have believed in this approach as well. Otherwise, why would he have depended so heavily on parables—stories about life—as the foundation of his approach to teaching? Indeed, as a pastor, I have been repeatedly humbled to find that few people remember the carefully structured thoughts and lines of reasoning upon which I painstakingly construct my sermons. Rather, they capture and recall the stories and analogies that illustrate the sermons, particularly the ones from the pages of my own life. Therefore, I have decided to present my thoughts about faith development largely through the medium of autobiographical writing.

I have chosen to use my own life as the canvas on which to paint a picture of faith development—not because my life is particularly unique, but because it is the story that I know best. Furthermore, it encompasses the chain of experiences which have given birth to my thoughts. I hope that you will see your own life and struggles in mine and that we can find kinship through this experience.

This book is divided into two major sections. The first section contains a series of glimpses into my life from childhood through the age of twenty-five. These glimpses or insights will, I hope, portray and personalize some of the issues involved in the struggle to develop Christian faith. As such, this first section is only subtly analytical. Its purpose is to tell a story, write a poem, or paint a picture that later will be more systematically assessed.

The second section of the book is for the purpose of analysis. Within these pages I will draw on the autobiographical account to point out and explain what I believe are nine major contributing factors to the development of Christian faith. These nine factors are the rivers that blend their waters into the lake of religious belief.

Recently, I read an article by Penrose St. Amant, a Southern Baptist pastor, missionary, and scholar. Dr. St. Amant made a statement that resonated within me as I feverishly tried to administer the program of a bustling church. He wrote, "We must always come back to the real meaning of success.

You don't measure Kingdom success by how much money a fellow raises, how many buildings he erects, how many books he writes, how many viewers or listeners or members he commands. You measure success by changed lives."[1] This book will be a success if it has a positive influence in the life of only one person.

As you read these chapters, it is my sincere prayer that God as Holy Spirit will be at work in your life and that your interaction with these pages will result in a deeper understanding of faith. Without this spiritual interaction, this book will be yet another volume collecting dust on a shelf.

I

THE RIVER'S COURSE

1

Reindeer Can't Fly

My earliest memories involve the church and people who professed belief in God. I don't want to be melodramatic, but as the son of a Baptist minister, I was practically born into the church—nurtured on the breast of faith and clothed in the garments of a cultural religion. My cradle was often a church pew; my lullaby a zestful congregational hymn of praise or thanksgiving. I learned prayers from the time I could talk and memorized Scripture along with Mother Goose.

For the most part I loved my churchhouse upbringing. I was spoiled by the attention I received because I was the "preacher's kid." And I enjoyed the impish childish rebellion I unleashed in Sunday school. I liked having a father who could address an audience and speak with authority. I looked forward to visiting the huge building in which God lived and where my daddy went to work every day.

As a child, however, I questioned the existence of God no more than a fish questions the water in which it is immersed. For, like the fish surrounded by water, I was surrounded by a community that believed in God. And in this fluid faith, I "lived and breathed and had my being."

Yet, even through the thickly woven fibers of this silken religious cocoon, an almost innate—but healthy—skepticism soon began to creep into my awareness. For within me there began to emerge a child-sized version of the ability to think critically. I began to ponder what had previously been the un-questionable.

Strangely, and yet understandably, my first critical religious thoughts had nothing to do with God, al-though they were profoundly theological. I will never forget that day when those fledgling thoughts pried themselves out of my pursed lips and flew into the outside world and into the presence of my father's hearing. These thoughts could no longer be kept a dark secret.

The day began with a practical joke. I climbed down out of my chair and scampered away from the breakfast table. My five-year-old mind had de-vised a plan that already had me laughing with glee as I ran through the living room to the front door. The Christmas bells that my mother had hung on the door jangled as I slammed it and ran outside. My father's big, black 1949 Hudson was parked in the driveway. Every day, he would get inside this monstrosity of a car and drive one mile to his church office.

On this particular day, I had decided that I was going to hide as a stowaway in the back seat of the car and surprise my father when we arrived at the church. So I carefully opened the heavy car door and lay flat on the rear floorboard while I waited for my father to come. After about five chilly minutes, I heard him whistling and crunching across the gravel. He got in the car, started the motor, and slowly backed down the driveway. When he shifted into drive and accelerated down the road, I knew my scheme had worked. I was so excited that I altered my plan to remain silent. At the next stoplight, I jumped up screaming like an Indian. We narrowly missed plowing into the car in front of us!

To say the least, this was quite a conversation starter. Chuckling to himself, my father decided not to take me back home but to let me spend the morning with him. I remember that as we drew closer to the church our conversation turned to the main topic of the season—Christmas—and I began to talk about my major preoccupation—Santa Claus.

"Dad, how do reindeer fly?" I asked as we pulled into the parking lot.

Turning off the ignition and slowly engaging the emergency brake, Dad fell silent. "Well, son, Santa has special reindeer. They're found only at the North Pole and no other place. Regular reindeer can't fly," he replied as he leaned back and looked at me, "but Santa's can."

For a moment I was quiet, and then the real issue

stammered forth: "Tommy says there ain't no Santa Claus. And he says reindeer can't fly."

Swallowing, Dad asked, "Well, what do you think? You know your buddy Tommy's not always right."

"I think he's right, Dad. Tommy's right. And Greg thinks so, too. Reindeer can't fly."

There was a deep silence. My father looked at me as never before—as if I were a different child, an older child. Slowly, he smiled and reached over and ruffled my red hair. "Don't you worry too much about Santa Claus," he said. "He'll get here, reindeer or no reindeer." But in his eyes I had seen his true reply. There was no Santa Claus and I knew it. Dad knew it. Tommy was right.

Strangely, I do not remember feeling any sadness at the realization of the death of poor Santa Claus. That grief was to come later on countless Christmas Eves when, even as an adult, I wanted to believe again in the mystical and fantastic magic of Santa Claus. But at that moment in the church parking lot, there was no sadness. For in the mirror of my father's long gaze, I had seen something new. Somehow I knew a secret had been disclosed that only older children and adults could share. (This was confirmed when my father later told me not to share our conversation with my little sister!) I knew that I was maturing, growing up. For, with a smile and a nod, I had just been granted membership into the fraternal order of those who do not believe in Santa Claus.

As we walked together into the church, Santa

Claus lay dying. But God was still in his heaven, and all was well on earth. Little did I know the depth of that day's discovery. Nor did I recognize that the seeds of skepticism had been planted. For with a smile, I had been set afloat on the awesome and powerful sea that rolls and surges between those two great shorelines—myth and reality. It is a sea I would spend a lifetime learning to navigate, to find my own course. For it was true—reindeer can't fly!

2

A Question in the Balcony

Santa died when I was five. Then, when I was six, my world changed—my father left the pastorate to become a theology professor in a faraway land. Appointed as a missionary to the Philippine Islands, he was to spend the remainder of his life teaching young Filipino seminarians systematic theology. Yet, he taught more than just seminarians; he also taught his son a great deal.

On Sunday mornings in the Philippines, I no longer saw my father standing center stage in an American pulpit. Instead, he soon became my Sunday school teacher. Gathered with five or six other American boys, I would listen while he taught us Bible stories. I don't remember exactly what he taught us; time and poor memory have compressed two or three years' worth of teaching into a hazy blur. But there is one exception, and that exception

stands out in my mind as clearly as if it were yesterday. That exceptional Sunday revolved around a lesson on the creation story in Genesis.

The setting for that Sunday was a bit unusual.
For lack of a better place, the small American community within the city where we lived had arranged
to use an old movie theater for an interdenomina-
tional Sunday school and worship service. My particular class of six- to eight-year-old boys met with my
father way up in the balcony of the theater.

By design, theaters are dark and cavernous, and
this one was musty as well. On one side of the theater
balcony was a huge window covered by a very thick
black curtain. On Sunday mornings, we drew back
the curtain and opened the window to let the cool
mountain breeze blow in. My father often sat on
the window sill while he taught us.

On this particular Sunday, when I was eight, I
was daydreaming as my father talked about the six
days of creation and the seventh day of rest. To
me the story was familiar; I had heard my mother
read it from children's Bible storybooks many times.
And I accepted it as totally true. I was far too young
to dabble in the complexities of literal versus figura-
tive truths. For me, Adam was a singular man and
Eve was a singular woman. The garden was in a geo-
graphical location. God was in his heaven and hu-
mankind was on the earth. I knew it all from
memory, and I believed it. It was as simple as the
pictures in the Bible storybook.

So, somewhat bored, I was looking out the window
up into the crystal blue of the sky—past my father

25

and far beyond the lesson. For some reason, I remember the crisp freshness of the breeze blowing across my face that day.

Then, in a split second, a lightning-bolt thought fell out of the sky and flashed across my mind. It was a thought that captivated and yet terrified me. It made the breeze and time—and even, I think, my heart—stop for a second. It was the deepest, most profound theological question that I have ever had, even to this day. With a sudden, direct urgency, I blurted out, "Who created God?"

There was that Santa Claus silence again, along with the feeling of coming of age. But this time there was not a wizened smile and a soft touch from my father. I barely remember what he said, but it was something about God's being eternal, infinite, the Alpha and Omega. I don't really recall his answer as being significant, but the question was forever burned on my mind.

Once again, I had crossed a significant threshold. I had grown older in a split second. I had joined the brotherhood of those who had questioned the origin of God. But there was no warm glow this time, no sense of proud accomplishment. There was only a subtle feeling of terror, of staring into the blue sky and suddenly being swallowed by a black hole in outer space. I had felt strangely good when Santa Claus had died. But I was enormously uncomfortable about questioning the origin of God.

Had I been an adult, I would have spent sleepless nights. I would have asked more questions. I would have looked at Sunday lunch and not felt hungry.

A Question in the Balcony

But, because I was a child, I left the question concerning the origin of God stuck with the bubble gum under the theater seat by the balcony window. I walked away and enjoyed Sunday lunch. But although with childish ability I postponed the quest for an answer, I never forgot the question. And the question never forgot me.

3

The Hammer of Life

Time passes rapidly in childhood and merges into the obscurity of days grown together. We lived in the Philippines for eight years. And, except for a few other "balcony" experiences, these were not *theological* years for me. In other words, I was not preoccupied with searching for God. Instead, I was preoccupied with school, sports, banter, and play.

During this period, however, I did make a public *profession of faith*, an important developmental step in the Baptist tradition. I was baptized. I attended church regularly. With twinges of guilt, I *rededicated my life* once or twice during revivals. These were all very significant and important experiences in my religious life. But they were not earthshaking theological experiences. They were not characterized by deep thinking about and the examination of my own religious faith. Rather, these special moments were more an inward and outward absorption of the religious heritage and tradition I had learned from my parents and my community.

This is not to say that my profession of faith and baptism were not meaningful to me in an intimate way! They were. But they were more signs of *accepting the faith that was my heritage* than of developing my own theology. I had not yet had to face the religious questions that come from the gale-force winds encountered later in life.

But the questions eventually came. They could not be avoided, for life has a way of forcing us to ask fundamental questions. My baptism into the deeper levels of life came at the tender, transitional, and awkward age of fourteen. At this age, a boy or girl has left behind the security of childhood but has not yet gained the defenses of an adult. These are vulnerable years.

When I was fourteen, my father became ill and we left the Philippines to return to America on a medical furlough. After a time of recuperation at my grandmother's home in Georgia, my family set off on a weekend trip to my father's former pastorate in South Carolina. On the way, we stopped for lunch in a small crossroads town. There, sitting at a table in a roadside restaurant, my father was suddenly stricken with a heart attack. There was no hospital to rush him to—only a small, three-room infirmary. To make matters worse, the town's only doctor could not be located by the sole nurse in charge of the infirmary.

As my father's condition became more critical by

the minute, and as his pain increased, a feeling of utter helplessness swept over me. Unless things improved quickly, my father—my innate symbol of the strength and dependability of life itself—was going to die. Yet there was nothing I could do except wait and sweat and pray.

Prayer came so naturally. I had been silently praying since we left the restaurant, but now I was becoming frantic. I felt that my silent prayers needed to be expressed more fervently. So I grabbed the hand of my ten-year-old sister and we left the room, leaving my mother alone with my father. I knew I had to find a place where I could pray seriously. I wanted to be alone with God, and the only available place was the infirmary bathroom. So I led her into what was to be our prayer closet.

I remember the bathroom floor—the white ceramic, diamond-shaped tile. I remember the coolness of the tile as we knelt on it. I recall the awkwardness of sharing my teenage vulnerability with my sister, of being open with my fear, of praying aloud in tones that more nearly resembled pleading than trust. And I remember having to finally say "Amen." Opening my brown eyes, I looked into her fearful blue ones.

As we walked back down the hall, the nurse met us. She didn't have to say anything; my mother's sobbing told us what had happened. The nurse embraced my sister and led her away. I walked into the room. I saw my mother bent over my father's body. His face was already turning blue.

I remember little else about that afternoon. But I do recall suddenly being in the room alone, the nurse having taken my mother aside. I stood stiffly and looked death in the face. Finally, I kissed my father on the cheek and pulled the bed sheet over his head. I was doing what I thought was expected of me. That was what they did in the movies. But in that act was symbolized more than I could ever know then and more than I can fully understand now. At the age of fourteen, I was experiencing stark tragedy for the first time. And I felt the electric anxiety that comes when a life characterized by order and control is suddenly thrown out of focus into chaos.

I gathered my father's clothing from a metal locker. I left the room to find that the clothes of a man did not fit a boy's frame. But I tried to wear them anyway. I thought I had no other choice.

Yet I had *prayed!* No one could have been more sincere. Still, Dad had died a horrible death. Where was God? Where was mercy? Where were the miracles and intercession? And why did God not answer my prayer? The hammer of life was suddenly pounding on the hard anvil of doubt and questioning. God was in his heaven, but all was no longer right with my world.

4

An Explosion in the Print Shop

And so, in my father's death, where was mercy for a fourteen-year-old boy? The mercy came in that I did not grow bitter, nor despairing, nor depressed. Somehow I chose to trust the goodness of God rather than to spit in his face.

Yet my perspective on God was changing. I knew that communication with him was not so simple as I once had thought. God was not Sears and Roebuck, a provider of all good things if I merely filled out the catalogue order form correctly. I now knew that evil and pain and loneliness were rampant in the world. God was in his heaven, but I was beginning to have a real problem with heaven!

After my father's death, my mother decided to settle in her hometown of Fort Valley. Nestled in the peach country of central Georgia, Fort Valley is small, quiet, and pleasant. In many respects, it

An Explosion in the Print Shop

is a typical Southern community. As the new kid
in town, having left behind all my friends and my
support system halfway around the world in the Philippines, I was in for my share of adjustments.

How did I find the stamina to bounce back from
my father's death and adjust to a completely new
way of life? I coped in the only way I knew how—
by staying very busy!

In this process of adjusting was born an adolescent
dream that was to affect my life for years to come.
My dream was to be what I called "well-rounded"—
to do many things well. I hoped to prove to myself
and to others that I was talented, energetic, and versatile. As such, I could roll, like a bouncing ball,
over the bumps and challenges of any terrain upon
which I tossed myself.

And so, through effort, I became increasingly well-
rounded. I rolled on faster and faster and faster. And
while on the fast track of those teenage years, I had
little time to think, or feel, or remember the past.

One of the most important aspects of being a well-
rounded American teenager is athletics. I came to
Georgia with a soccer ball under my arm, only to
exchange it for a strange, oblong football. I didn't
know a scrimmage line from a huddle nor a quarter-
back from a center; nevertheless, I learned to play
the game. My one-hundred-forty pounds usually rel-
egated me to the bench. But I made the team, earned
my letter, got my picture in the school annual, and
fed my ego.

In the spring, I played on the tennis team and
did fairly well. I also tried out for basketball, only

to find I had little aptitude for the game. And so I became only somewhat well-rounded in an athletic sense. I learned to play all the games, although I mastered none.

And yet, I did not want to be seen as a "jock." I wanted very much to be versatile. I became involved on the debate team and loved the competition of debate tournaments. I found that, although I often didn't know what I was talking about, I could always talk. And then there was drama and music. Participation in these activities helped me to overcome my biggest fear—stage fright! I soon found I enjoyed singing in choruses and quartets. And I fell in love with Broadway musicals. My mother grew quite weary of my coming home at midnight from a date or a night on the town bellowing, "Oh, What a Beautiful Morning." I loved to sing, to act, to talk—to express myself.

Somewhat strangely, my quest to become well-rounded did not include academics. I was quite content to stay in the middle of the pack, to coast along—even to flunk one year of algebra. There were other more important things than study; there were brighter worlds to conquer. And so, when football practice ended, one-act play rehearsals were dismissed, and all the organized activities I embraced ground to a standstill, I would go home and sit nervously at my desk with my books. But this seldom lasted longer than five minutes before one of the Marlboro Crew would show up and rescue me.

The Marlboro Crew was a great bunch of guys. Even though I was one of the few in the Marlboro

An Explosion in the Print Shop

Crew who attended church regularly, we were all brothers in a faith directed toward finding—among other things—meaning in life.

Our search usually involved a set routine. Around eight o'clock in the evening, one of us would get a car and pick up the rest of the crew. Feeling secure and cocky in each other's company, we would head for the Tastee-Freeze, the center of a teenager's universe in small Georgian towns.

At "The Freeze," we were always sure there would be beautiful damsels awaiting us, longing to be spirited away from the dragons of boredom. And so we would ride around the parking lot in ceremonious circles waiting for the girl of our dreams. We ate ice cream to cool our fantasies and created today's gas shortage by our incessant circling. After an hour, we usually left, because the girls seldom showed. Or, if they did, they were the same old ones. Unfortunately, variety was not the spice of our lives.

Upon leaving The Freeze, we quit riding in circles and returned to discover anew every square inch of our town. We would ride down every street thinking of practical jokes to play. My innovative specialty was devising stunts we had never pulled before. We kept the toilet paper industry alive by "rolling" trees and houses and kept the spray-paint industry solvent by "customizing" the water tower. We set strangely misplaced outhouses on the front steps of the high school. On occasion, we threw an egg or two. Once, after midnight, we even played over the loudspeaker system of the Methodist church a sound-effects record of jets flying overhead and dropping bombs.

Startled neighbors were convinced that the Russians were coming. And although the police were convinced that we were the culprits, they couldn't prove it.

When we became bored with rediscovering our town, we would set out for the countryside. But before we could leave, we always had to stop at the gas station for a pack of Marlboro cigarettes. We just could not navigate the dark countryside without the warmth and glow of Marlboros. There was a reason for this, however. When we circled the Tastee-Freeze, we dreamed about and spoke of girls. When we cruised through town, we focused our attention on practical jokes. But when we departed to the countryside and the street lights faded away, sooner or later our conversation became philosophical. And to talk philosophically, we felt we simply had to have Marlboros.

Cruising through the darkness, we talked about the Vietnam War and how we might all join the Marines when we graduated from high school. We talked about UFO's and were even sure we saw one late one night. Sometimes we talked about God and whether or not he existed. We usually agreed that he did—belief in God somehow seemed to have a lot to do with joining the Marines.

But while it was all profoundly interesting, it was not profoundly *personal*. I never talked about the grief I was experiencing as a result of my father's death. I never shared the fact that, because I was raised in the Philippines, I could identify with the displaced ancestors of the black citizens segregated

36

on the other side of town. I never talked about the girl I had loved dearly but had to leave behind. And I found that I was not the only one who exhaled my pain in the silent cigarette smoke. One night my best friend hyperventilated; we thought he was dying. Later, the doctor explained that his condition was the result of his being too uptight over a recent breakup with his girlfriend. None of us knew he even had a girlfriend!

There was a lot we just didn't know how to say to each other. And yet, there was an awkward intimacy in the fact that we sat silently together in those cars and rescued each other from home and from books. We were intimate because we shared our sports and our pranks and our cigarettes and our dreams.

Every night, we returned home around midnight. If I was not driving my mother's car, my friends would let me out where the driveway met the street. Then, with a kick of gravel, the Crew would be gone. As their fading headlights rounded the corner at the end of the street, I would turn to face our darkened house. (Mom never sat up waiting for me. She trusted me far more than I trusted myself.)

As I ambled down the driveway to the house, I almost always walked into the backyard for a few fleeting minutes. These were sacred moments—the rare times in my teenage years when I was alone.

In our yard were huge pecan trees, and behind our rear hedge grew acres and acres of peach trees. I would either walk slowly between the trees or slouch in a lawn chair. Inevitably, I would look up at the night sky, for it has always held my deepest fascination. It has been my cathedral, my high-vaulted place of worship; my dark blanket which has brought me the warmth of God. Conversely, it has also been the eternal stage on which I have been brought into interplay with the stark fear and awe of the Holy. Before laying down to rest an over-extended teenager's body, I was always drawn to the sky.

The constellation Orion became my good friend. With his star-studded belt and sword, he cut away my emotional defenses. I could talk personally with him. But behind Orion was something greater, something I could not see. There was a cosmic mystery that often caused me in the silence of my midnight reverie to whisper the words of the psalmist:

When I consider thy heavens,
the work of thy fingers,
the moon and the stars,
which thou hast ordained;
What is man, that thou art mindful of him?
and the son of man, that thou
visitest him? (8:3–4, KJV)

Somehow the night sky pulled my head up to where I had always felt God was—in the sky, in the heavens, behind Orion and all the other stars. And for a few seconds I felt a mystical union with God. I experienced a reassurance of his reality that paradoxically brought me to exclaim reverently, "What is man, that thou art mindful of him?"

An Explosion in the Print Shop

It was on such a night during my private time that, for a moment, I lost my sense of direction as my mind wandered between the trees and up into space. I lost my way following the circuitry of an age-old thought. And suddenly, I feared I could never find my way home again.

Only moments before, I had been with the Marlboro Crew, and someone had mentioned an interesting piece of trivia as we thundered back into town. A few minutes later, in my cathedral of stars, that one little fact became earthshaking for me. One of my friends had read that the light which we perceived that very night from some of the more distant stars had actually been emitted before the birth of Christ. It had taken the starlight we were now seeing nearly two thousand years to travel through the void of space to our receptive eyes.

Mentioned in the car, this was interesting trivia. Now, alone with Orion, I was awestruck by the immensity of it all.

I knew from my science courses that light travels 186,000 miles—nearly seven times the circumference of the earth—in one second. I knew that it takes light only eight minutes to travel from the sun to the earth and that, in a year, light travels approximately six trillion miles. My mind reeled at just the thought of one light year, much less two thousand light years.

Suddenly, God fell out of his heaven—or, at least, heaven as I had always envisioned it. With jarring abruptness, I could no longer with integrity think of God in a physical or spatial way. Indeed, I could

39

hardly think of God at all, for to think human thoughts was to enter the realms that could not contain him—space and time and the physical. In the course of a few seconds, I rationally and emotionally discovered that God did not live above the clouds, above the earth, "above" anything—any more than reindeer could fly. And yet I knew that I still tenaciously believed in God, because I felt him—because I simply *knew* he existed.

In fact, the argument that had just sent my mind reeling was part of the reason I still believed in God. As I sat under those trees, looking at the stars and the boundlessness of space, I thought about the organ that made my experience with starlight possible—my eyes. I reflected on the intricacies of the human eye. I considered the complexities of my body, of society, of the physical world, and of the universe. These thoughts welled up in me as if they were a new-found discovery, and I savored the absolute order, precision, and miracle of creation. I innately sensed that behind creation must be a Creator, that behind physical order must be ultimate order, that behind time and space there must be an ultimate time and space so profound that we can hardly conceive of them.

All these thoughts of ultimacy overwhelmed me. All I knew on that night was that somehow the order of it all—the immensity of it all—made me believe that there is a God. But I could not verbalize my thoughts any more than I could hurl a stone and hit a star.

Much later in my life, I came across the writings

of Leslie Weatherhead, who put into words what I felt on that night:

> If there is no purposefulness to be found in the universe, then it is the result of a colossal accident, and, as Edwin Conklin the biologist said, "The probability of life originating from accident is comparable to the probability of the unabridged dictionary resulting from an explosion in a printing shop."[1]

I do not believe that the unabridged dictionary came by accident. Nor could I believe, at that time of my life, that the immensity of space and the order of the universe happened by accident. And so I held firm to my belief in God, the Creator.

But there had been a colossal explosion that night in the print shop of my mind. For though I still believed in God, my conceptualization process had been blown away. I could not tell you *who* God was, nor *what* he was, nor *where* he was, nor even if he was indeed a "he." I could only say, "God is—God exists."

I went to bed that night disturbed, perplexed, and—to be quite honest—frightened. But I was more in love with God, the awesome God of the void, than ever before. In looking at the sky, I had sensed, though not seen, the face of God. I had seen his shadow. And Orion had smiled!

5

Squeezed

Like the cigarettes we smoked, the flames of youth could not burn forever. Time ran out for the Marlboro Crew. Our demise was symbolized by the large senior rings on our fingers and the graduation tassels we hung on the rear-view mirrors of our cars.

We hoped we would not drift apart; we vowed silently that we wouldn't. But we all did go our separate ways. One became the town's mortician; one left to work in industry; one became a business executive. And one left town to become an actor, a politician, a doctor, a quixotic humanitarian; then, after having given up on all four quests, became none of them and all of them—a preacher. And that was me. But had you told me as a senior in high school that ordination was what the future held for me six years hence, I certainly would have joined the

Marines. I had no ambition nor desire to become a pious man of the cloth.

But leave town I did. I gleefully departed to attend Furman University in Greenville, South Carolina. Nestled at the foot of the Appalachian Mountains and built around a picturesque lake, Furman is an excellent Baptist liberal arts school. I did not, however, choose Furman for its academics. I chose it because it had a beautiful campus, pretty girls, a soccer team, and a drama department. Also, my best friend from the Philippines had received an academic scholarship to Furman, and we had vowed to attend college together. (Varied and strange are often our reasons for making major decisions in life.)

As I stood holding the last suitcase taken from the trunk of the car and watched my mother and sister drive away after depositing me at my college dormitory, I sensed that a major new chapter was being opened in my life, and an old and familiar one was quickly closing. I was consciously aware of wanting to place a bookmark right there in the pages of my days, so that I might be able to reread the last chapter again. But I also knew that, although I might reread it, the chapter had been written and must stand as it was. This chapter was the story of my childhood, of my adolescence, of living under the same roof with one family, one history, and a common faith. I would revisit this chapter and reread it many times, but I could add nothing to its pages.

As I turned to take my suitcase to my room, the taste in my mouth was both bitter and sweet—but mostly sweet, because I was excited to be on my own! Even though the umbilical cord had not been completely severed, I knew that I was being born into another world—the adult world.

I quickly unpacked my well-rounded self and began to bounce around new terrain—the college campus. I soon found that there were other people much better-rounded than I, and that I didn't roll as quickly or as smoothly as I had in Fort Valley. In other words, I found what most kids from a small town discover—that a big fish in a small bowl becomes a small fish when put in a big bowl. On the whole, that was all right with me; I needed and wanted new challenges and room to expand. However, the hurt of realizing my limitations is a growing pain that I never relished. To grow wiser is to grow humbler. And most of the wisdom I developed during my college years was the kind that comes not from a growing intellect, but from a forced—yet more honest and refined—reappraisal of myself.

My first few months of college were characterized by a familiar and recurring theme of *making it.* I made my way onto the soccer team and into the drama guild and chorale. I made new friends in the dorm and new girlfriends with whom to sit in the library and walk around the lake late at night. I also made two Ds and one C on my first grade report and was promptly put on academic probation.

Nevertheless, I was happy and content. Unfortunately, I was also broke. I did not know how to manage my limited allowance. I sorely missed my mother's charge accounts at the clothing store, filling station, grocery store, and drug store. I was, indeed, receiving a liberal education.

By Christmas, I knew some things had to change. The word *priority* was developing a more defined and important meaning in my life. I decided I would not play soccer until my grades improved. I became inactive in the drama guild. I chose to focus on my classes, the chorale, and the heady wine of dating— in inverse order. I also decided I must get a job in order to stay in school, for in those years dropping out of college meant being drafted by the armed services and sent to Vietnam. (Now that joining the Marines was a real option and not just a high-school escape fantasy, I began to let my hair grow longer and to take conscientious objection to war a little more seriously.)

In the midst of my struggle with priorities, I began to feel pressure to declare an academic major. Although I was content simply to take the courses my academic advisor suggested, every official university form I filled out wanted to know my name, my social security number, and my declared major. Every person I met asked me where I was from and what my major was. I was beginning to realize that I could not have an acceptable identity without a declared academic major. At the same time, I hesitated because of the claustrophobic feeling that, once I declared a major on an academic form, I was destined for all time to walk in the ruts of that vocation. (I knew that this was not true, but the feeling nevertheless haunted me.) But the pressure was building, and a decision was called for.

I found that such decisions are usually made through a process of elimination. One course of chemistry convinced me that medicine was out. My political career dimmed after one good dose of political science. And even though I was still infatuated by drama, I could soon see that my name was not destined to be seen in lights on Broadway; I did not have the singularity of vision and devotion necessary to develop the required dramatic skills.

I began to sense that the nondefined vocational path on which I was walking was developing a thin layer of ice. I felt as though I was slipping, falling down, not making progress. I began to reach out and grasp for something that I had always called "God's will for my life."

Timidly, I started to spend some time in hurried but serious prayer asking God to reveal his special will for my life. I made it quite clear in my prayers that I was prepared to do anything God wanted me to do if he would only plainly direct me and clearly reveal his will. I thought my proposition was very fair—even heroic. But although God was given a good opportunity to acquire another faithful disciple—indeed, a martyr—he was strangely silent. Or at least God was silent in the ways that I expected him to be vocal and upfront with me. I had assured him in no uncertain terms that I would follow him.

Squeezed

All that I expected was a pillar of fire to guide me through my vocational night. Instead, I was left staring at a cloud-covered moon and overcast stars.

Naturally I became frustrated. I had talked fervently to God, and he hadn't answered—or so it seemed.

Now, as I look back, I realize that I had not yet learned to listen to a Voice that speaks most truly in the syllables of silence. I had not attuned myself to hear a Voice that speaks when we are ready to listen rather than when we are ready to pray. I had not learned to listen with the ears of faith and not just to the sounds of reason. God *was* speaking, but I was praying so loudly that I heard only the echoes of my own voice.

I can see now that God did not try to break through my frustration and confusion. God (if I can give him such human qualities) did not shout the directions that I was asking for over the din of my own noise. He did not remove my frustration and confusion. Rather, he *used* my frustration and confusion to prod me forward.

I was becoming clay in God's hands. But the potter's wheel on which I was being turned was constructed from the rough-hewn timbers of searching and frustration and confusion. God was turning me and molding me, but I didn't like the dizziness of that experience. I wanted to be instantly poured into a mold. I did not want to be slowly formed and shaped and caressed over time by the creative hands of God. I wanted to be well-rounded, to be able to roll on all terrain, to give up nothing nor close the door to any options. Instead, the Creator's hands were gently squeezing me, shaping me, making my edges more linear and well-defined. He was deflating a bouncing ball and remaking it into a more open, receptive, usable vessel.

6

Between the Barn and the Fence

After the first semester of college, finding a job became an increasingly pressing issue. My mother was quite willing to continue to foot my bills through loans and sacrificial giving on her part. But there was something within me that was finding this arrangement increasingly hard to swallow.

I was concerned about my mother; I didn't want her teaching school every day and constantly worrying about how she would make ends meet. But more than worrying about my mother, I was concerned about my own ego. I wanted to cut the apron strings and be independent. I wanted to be a man. And I had been raised on my father's depression-era philosophy that being a man meant paying one's own bills. I, therefore, decided to enter the job force. And the next decision that confronted me was "What job?"

Now, I don't think I am lazy by nature. I have

always worked very hard on activities and pursuits in which I am interested and motivated. In college, I had certainly worked diligently in the "making it" department! But the idea of working hard just to acquire money did not exactly turn me on. I had never been hungry; consequently, I was lazy in this area. I looked for the easiest job I could find.

I could have gotten a job in the school cafeteria; however, I felt this was too messy and time consuming. The college post office was hiring students, but I didn't like the hours. And any kind of work during the week would mean dropping intramural sports, the chorale, and much pleasurable goofing off—a sacrifice I was not willing to make. So I decided I needed a weekend job.

One day I happened upon the college chaplain, a very likeable fellow, and he asked me how things were going. During the course of the conversation, I mentioned that I was looking for a job. He replied that the church he attended was looking for a youth director and asked whether I would be interested.

I told him I would think about it. But *thinking* about the position wasn't as important as how I *felt* about it. And a big part of me said, "No!"

For eighteen years, I had been dutifully going to church every single Sunday of the year. Now, at last, I was calling my own shots. As a result, during the first six months of college, I had rarely attended church. There was something about sleeping in on Sunday mornings that was absolutely delightful. It was great to turn off the alarm clock and wearily fall back into the embrace of warm covers while others rushed for the showers. A few of us would haughtily joke during Sunday lunch that we had attended "Saint Mattress Baptist Church" that morning.

I was not really rebelling nor reacting against my past—although there was an element of reaction. Primarily, I was just resting from eighteen years of a forced march back and forth through the church doors. I was now trying to catch my breath, to set my own pace for a change. I was taking a sabbatical from the regimen of habit and tradition.

This was a primary reason that I bridled at the thought of being a youth director, of working for a church, of having to be there every Sunday. And if I *did* go to church, I wanted to attend out of my own desire, not from the dictates of a job description. But, besides this, there was an even deeper factor involved—a factor that really spooked me. Quite simply, I did not want to end up being a preacher.

Preachers' kids are inevitably in tension with their preacher-parent and his (or her) pastoral identity. This *double-bind* form of tension comes out of a love-hate relationship, a relationship I had experienced most of my life.

I deeply loved and respected my father. He was a man of great courage and boundless energy. And when he placed the "yoke of Christ" across his shoulders, that energy was translated into a driving conviction, a relentless devotion to the good news of the gospel. His life had a purpose. He stood for something, and his life was not wasted. Dad was characterized by quality, and I admired that.

But there was another side to the picture, a side that bothered me. As my father put on the yoke and began dutifully to plow the "fields white unto harvest," he also lost something. Some of the fierceness left him; the tossing mane and independent gait of a wild stallion disappeared. He became domesticated, fed and sheltered in the barn of the church and fenced in somewhat by the expectations of a Bible-belt society. And although he never lost his strength and passion, he did lose some of his ability to bound freely and roam relentlessly wherever he pleased.

The domestication of a pastor can be a problem for his or her children—children who have not freely chosen the yoke of God, yet must live with their parents in the ecclesiastical barn. The constrained preacher's kids feel, as all children do, the call of the wild, but they view it through the slats of a barnyard fence. They want to run across the plains with other liberated colts until they run out of breath and ache with exertion. Yet the minister's children know that they must first grow tall and strong enough in their own right to hurdle over the corral fence.

As a college student, I remembered many nights not so long past in high school when I leaned longingly against that corral fence but was not yet strong enough to jump over it. Often that experience took place after football games at the local American Legion Hall where we held our high-school dances. Some two-bit band from Americus or Macon would be playing, but the quality of their sound really didn't matter. We were there to laugh loudly, to mingle, and to dance. It was always the scene of great fun.

For me, however, it was often the scene of being uncomfortable and embarrassed. I did not dance. And my reluctance to dance did not come from either timidity nor big feet, but from the fact that my deceased father and, therefore, my mother did not believe in dancing. Their conservative Baptist mindset dictated that dancing excited one's animal lusts and led directly to unwed pregnancies and broken homes. And though my mother, in a confessional moment, did tell me once that when she was in high school she would rather have danced "than eat," dancing was still not something in which a Walker participated. And so, rather than dance, I stood around.

There is nothing more humiliating than to lean up against a wall at a dance as if it were your assigned responsibility to keep the roof from falling in. Worse yet is to have a date who wants to dance—and to have to mumble something about not believing in dancing, or pretend you have an injured ankle, or tell some other lie. All the while, you know you are mouthing an ethical code that is not your own. And to add insult to injury, there is always some guy who will smoothly come up and ask to dance with your date. It is galling to see the coy pleasure on her face as she glides by.

My mother must have sensed my frustration. One day she walked into the den and exclaimed, "Scott, I know what goes on at those dances, and I guess if you must choose between smooching in a parked car or dancing, I'd rather have you dance." When she put the situation in that light, I finally had my own defensible reason for not wanting to dance!

But dance I finally did when I went to college, although not out of true choice. During my freshman year, a guy on my hall lined up three of us with blind dates for the homecoming game and dance. These girls were from a "high society" private school in Charleston. I will never forget the moment as we stood in front of the girls' dorm waiting to pick up our dates. They were late and hadn't arrived from Charleston yet. As we paced nervously looking at our watches, a large black Cadillac came screeching around the curve and came to a stop in front of the dorm. A chauffeur jumped out, opened the back door, and three glamorous young women emerged. My friend had set us up well. Too well!

The thought hit me like a brick. How was I ever going to tell this beautiful young thing that I didn't dance when I had knowingly consented to take her to a dance? Throughout the ballgame I worried about what I was going to do. And though I thought of a dozen excuses for not dancing, they all sounded as lame and false as I knew they were. I realized that I was going to have to "face the music"—literally. My decision was confirmed when my date sweetly told me that there was nothing she would rather do than dance. So, seeing that this was definitely a case of situation ethics, I danced and danced and loved it. Fortunately for me, in my era of college, there was no such thing as correct dance steps. All one had to do was move in a discombobulated fashion. I could do that very well.

So, symbolically, the young colt had jumped the corral fence. And although I can't even remember her name, I'll always thank that girl from Charleston for the gentle nudge.

Yet once a colt gains the courage to jump the fence (whatever the fence may be), he is not easily coaxed back into the barnyard. Suddenly aware of his freedom, he usually has to kick his heels a bit, to rear back his head and loudly neigh, to jump and bound and race until he is salty and lathered. Only when he is taxed and hungry will the colt approach the fence again and contemplate the hay inside.

I was beginning to feel hungry. I had cleared the fence and run my race and fortunately, had not chosen to leave the safe pasture for the deeper woods. I had grown stronger from the boundless runs and, except for a few scratches from brambles and briars, I was none the worse from the experience.

But now dusk was falling and the barnyard beckoned. Was I willing to be a youth director? Was I that hungry for financial support, for the familiar, for a sense of doing something worthwhile?

After a few days of thought, I went to see the chaplain and told him I was willing to at least talk about the job with the pastor and youth committee from the church. Then, when I met the committee, I became excited about what they wanted me to do. I couldn't believe someone wanted to pay me to coach softball teams, to direct religious dramas, to plan hikes and outings—in short, just to be a big brother to a lot of junior-high and high-school kids. And I could do it all on weekends!

I accepted the job as soon as it was offered. But I asked God to accept something, too. I asked him to honor a deep-felt wish, a wish that can best be expressed by a memory.

The first Sunday night that I was officially the youth director of the church, there was a fellowship to welcome me on board after the evening service. It made me feel warm and loved and excited. Following the fellowship, I lingered in the parking lot telling the last of the kids good-bye and watching as the final car disappeared.

Having turned off the last light and locked the church door, I was suddenly alone in the darkened parking lot. I turned to look up again at my friend Orion. I felt good. But I also felt uneasy, and from deep within me the words tumbled out:

Thank you, Father. Thank you for taking care of my needs. And thank you for this church and my job. But please, Father, please don't ask me to be a preacher. Just use this job to train me to be a dedicated layman, a youth worker. But God, please, I just don't want to be a preacher!

I was being honest. The young colt was within the corral again, but he was standing outside the barn, straining his neck through the door and hungrily eating hay from within. It tasted good. But I did not want to venture inside the barn. I was safe within the corral, but I knew I could jump the fence at will. If I entered the barn, there was always the chance that somebody might slam the door and lock it. And I feared that somebody would be God!

7

A Little Knowledge

I was back in the fold—the all-American youth director. Leading Bible studies, modeling Christian character, smiling brightly, wearing bell-bottom jeans (the youth uniform of the day). I think I must have exuded a noticeable air of confidence, if not cockiness. But the confidence was much on the outside, for on the inside, my traditional Christianity was being shaken by a new challenge that the old Marlboro Crew had never dreamed of.

The shakiness came from a new course I was taking entitled "An Introduction to Biblical Literature." As a senior in high school, I had reckoned myself to be a biblical authority. As a college sophomore, I now knew I was nothing of the sort. I was facing the fact that I knew very little about how the Bible was written or about its very nature and literary character. And my lack of knowledge alarmed me.

For years I had heard disturbing things about college religion professors. I had listened since childhood to stories about ivory-tower atheists who covertly infiltrated denominational colleges and took sadistic delight in ripping away the young and vulnerable faith of their naïve students. And hearing was now believing.

At times, I truly wondered if my Bible course was being taught by a likeable devil incarnate. Indeed, when he told the class that Genesis was not written word for word by Moses, nor were all of the Psalms composed by David, I was almost sure of it. Yet the horns never quite popped out, and he always left the pitchfork outside the door. In fact, I later came to see him as a pretty neat old fellow with a passionate love for God and a zeal to deepen the faith of his students. But for awhile, I thought he was the devil.

For me, the Bible had always been "the Word of God." That meant that God wrote it and I believed it—it was that simple. And although I had always known that it was man who set "pen to paper" and wrote Genesis and Psalms and the Gospel of Mark and Revelation, I had always pictured these men as being something like first-grade students with big pencils in their little hands, copying diligently word for word what God wrote on the blackboard. And if there was any problem or confusion, God would place his big hand over their little hands and guide their pencils. That, I thought, was the way the Bible was written.

I found out this wasn't true. For I was led to ask

myself where the big blackboard was from which they copied God's writing. Was it in the sky or in the sands of the desert? I knew better. I had to admit it was written on human hearts and in the mortal minds of men of old. I also had to admit that I didn't like thinking this way. I wanted my Bible, my source for religious authority, to be God's word verbatim, not man's understanding of God's word. I did not want it to be man's word about God, even if these men of old were powerfully inspired by God's Holy Spirit. I wanted a blackboard in the room on which the Bible was written. I discovered there was not one.

This new realization stayed with me at all hours—it hounded and threatened me. If I could not believe that God literally dictated every word of the Bible to men who recorded it as stated, could I believe the Bible at all? Was God big enough and strong enough to communicate his holy truth in mortal fashion, through mortal thought, through human expression and grammatical errors and Pauline temper tantrums? I wasn't really sure God was that big. And I wasn't sure if I was big enough to face my questions.

All my turmoil came to a climax late one night. Staring into the close darkness of a ceiling three feet from my nose, I felt my roommate restlessly tossing in the bunk beneath me. It was 3:30 A.M. For several hours I had tried to sleep, but I couldn't switch off my mind. I felt my whole body racing like a car engine with its idle out of balance. Yet even

60

though I couldn't sleep, I was exhausted—tired of thinking and tired of trying not to think. I was afraid that my faith in God was going to be ripped away. In the darkness, I felt like an astronaut, floating in space, who suddenly realizes that all the support lines connecting him to the security of the home capsule are being severed. I sensed it was my questions about the authority of Scripture that were cutting my support lines, and I feared I would be left to drift until my death, lost in the void of unbelief.

I gave up on sleep. I slid quietly off my top bunk and groped for my old silk robe, which I had inherited years ago from my uncle. It had dragged the ground when I first wore it, but now my six-foot frame filled it snugly. I had hidden in its shelter many times, its thick silkiness never failing to warm me. And though it was now frayed and worn, I reached for it like a child seeking a security blanket.

I stood still for a moment, hearing only the sounds of my roommate's relaxed breathing and the heated gurgling of an old metal radiator. Then I quietly opened the door and walked down the hall.

A men's dormitory is a strange place at half-past three in the morning. Outside, it was sleeting. But inside, there was the warm, hushed stillness of a nursery at night. A hundred or more boyish men breathed in unison, cradled in bunks and blankets, spinning tomorrow's dreams and repressing yesterday's regrets. For a few brief hours, all were hushed children again.

As my bare feet shuffled against the cold tile of the hallway, I longed for that warm and carefree sleep I, too, had known only a few nights before. I walked past my best friend's room, and for a moment, I thought about knocking and waking him to share my thoughts and anxiety. But I didn't. Some thoughts are too big for words. If I expressed them to him at all, I felt it would be in the silence that only intimate friends can share or with tears I was not yet mature enough to cry. So I walked on.

At the end of the hall was a window, a vantage point, a place to stop and look out upon a winter world. The sleet was changing to snow. Not far away was a streetlight—a solitary candle. I watched as the snow and sleet danced around the light like moths about a flame and as the cold wet ground became covered with a powdered whiteness.

Leaning against the window sill, I found my mind was lulled into a hush, as silent as snowflakes touching the earth. For a while there was no time. The pendulum had stopped. There was no ticking, no movement of gears and cogs and arms. Only a hushed silence.

Then, through the silence, a voice slowly surfaced in my mind. It was my father's voice, speaking in quiet and reasoned tones. Where or when my child's mind had recorded this verbal memory I do not know. No original scene or situation can now be visualized. But the words were there, loud and clear.

The voice said, "If you learn a little about religion, it will be enough to turn you to atheism. But if you pursue your study of God for a long time, you will inevitably find faith."

The snow continued to fall. Time began again. I sensed that what Dad had said was true. The little I knew about theology and biblical studies *was* tripping me up, confusing me, threatening me. Now I had a clear choice to make.

I could walk away from it all, drop my class, and close my mind. I had not gone so far on my pilgrimage of seeking deeper truth and new light that I could not turn around and run back to unquestioned beliefs and to the sanctity of tradition. I could go back.

But there was another choice—and that was to forge ahead. I could choose to continue to study and read and critically appraise my religious-belief structure with the mind of reason and the eyes of faith. This way was a perilous choice—a road to the unknown with road signs that could only be read through the rear-view mirror. And the destination was mine alone if I chose to take a step in that direction. That was the decision I had to make—to take a step backward or forward. If I took the step forward, I could never go home again. The bridge would be burned.

Sometimes in life we are pushed. At other times we are drawn. On that night, I was drawn forward by what I can only call the gentle grace of God. I made the decision to continue on, to move forward instead of retreating to guard the gates of parental faith. There was a promise of nothing. Only a presence, the drawing presence of God.

A decision was made. Tired, but now not weary, I dropped my head and heard the words come forth from my lips, "Father, give me the faith that I will find faith." It was as honest as I could be. And there was an inaudible answer: "Come, follow me."

8

Meeting Dr. Freud

At the end of my sophomore year, I was faced with a decision as to whether or not I was going to continue studying at Furman University. As usual, there were two sides to consider carefully.

On the positive side, I wanted to stay. I loved Furman. I had a great set of friends, and I found I was really enjoying my history and religion courses. Indeed, after deciding to dive into the pool of religious study, I discovered that I could not only dog paddle and flounderingly survive; I could actually swim and enjoy it. The "old devil" professors had become friends. The fear for the most part had gone. I was challenged to continue.

But on the negative side, my steady girlfriend was transferring to nursing school in Georgia, and my heart told me I could not survive the bite of separation. In addition, there was a math course at Furman that one must pass if one expected to graduate. I had flunked it twice, and I saw no glimmer of hope on the horizon. Furthermore, I was still struggling financially. Not being on a scholarship, I was finding myself taking out loans to pay tuition. All of this made me uneasy.

So a decision was at hand and, for better or worse, I decided to transfer to Mercer University in Macon, Georgia. Like Furman, Mercer is a Baptist school with an excellent religion department. And Mercer, in one of their weaker moments, decided to extend me a scholarship. It was given not because of my grades and academic performance, but because I just happened to have graduated from a high school in a region of the state from which Mercer was trying to attract students. (God watches over fools and little children!)

During my sophomore year at Furman, I had finally made the official decision to major in Asian-African studies. I felt that such an academic background would help me prepare to work with the United Nations or a relief agency concerned with the development of deprived Third World countries. This was where my interest and vocational yearnings were leading me. I sincerely wanted to help people who could not help themselves.

I had always been something of an idealistic humanitarian. I now found that my childhood experiences in the Philippines were becoming a formative force in my emerging adult consciousness. But I did not want to be a minister nor a missionary; I still balked at entering the ecclesiastical barn again. The

United Nations or the Peace Corps seemed like a breath of fresh air. Churches and barns did not. So I began to prepare myself to be a Christian witness through a secular organization.

I forgot to do one important thing, however. I neglected to check whether Mercer had an Asian-African studies program before I transferred! I simply assumed that they did. They did not.

Sheepishly holding a college catalogue that I should have consulted before—not after—I transferred, I again found myself floating without an academic major and a sense of direction. Feeling as if I needed to talk to someone, I went to see the only Mercer professor I knew. She happened to be head of the psychology department. And in the course of the conversation, she suggested that I enroll in a psychology course she was teaching.

I had considered studying psychology before, but I had always hesitated to do so. On the one hand, I loved the study of human nature; people had always been my greatest source of interest. In this respect, I was naturally attuned to the science of psychology. But on the other hand, I had always feared that psychology would make me look not just at other people, but at myself as well—that it would strip me of my protective clothing and force me to stand emotionally naked in front of the mirror of self-examination and introspection.

I wasn't sure I wanted to take off my protective emotional covering. I was afraid I might see something I didn't want to face. I wasn't sure what that something was. But I sensed, in honest moments, that there was a part of me from which I wanted to hide.

Partly because I knew I was afraid of it, I decided to take the psychology course. I couldn't bear to admit I was intimidated, so I thrust myself into it. And it wasn't as bad as I had thought. Experimental psychology dealt mostly with rats and pigeons, and I could handle that.

It wasn't until much later, when I took a course in psychopathology and looked into the mirror of the human psyche, that I became a little unhinged. I had always known there was a little crazy in me. What I didn't know is that there is a little crazy in everybody. When I took psychopathology, I began to look at my crazy side. Suddenly, I related in some way to the symptoms of almost every form of mental and emotional illness that we studied. Like a first-year medical student, I developed every disease we discussed. I became a psychological hypochondriac. I found I had neurotic characteristics. I even had a few schizophrenic, manic depressive, obsessive-compulsive, and hysterical tendencies as well. I didn't like all this. I wanted to be totally and wholly normal. Over time, however, I began to realize that there is no such thing as a "normal" person. We are all a mixture of the healthy and the neurotic and the crazy. I didn't like it, but I had to face it: Since there are no "normal" people, I couldn't be "normal." I had to be Scott Walker, whoever he was. Perhaps he wasn't "normal," but he wasn't crazy, either.

One cannot study psychology very long without

coming face-to-face with a little bearded man named Sigmund Freud, the "papa" of modern psychology. The shadow of Freud falls across the path of every psychology student. The student doesn't ever have to *agree* with Freud. But to enter into a personal dialogue and debate with him is unavoidable.

My own debate with Freud came over the issue of the existence of God. Freud was a Jew. As a child, he was taught about the God of the Old Testament. But as an adult and a scientist, he began to doubt God's existence. Perhaps, he thought, the God hidden above the clouds exists only in the faithful minds of bearded old rabbis. And so Freud postulated that God is only a mental projection caused by a growing child's yearning for a father figure lost in childhood, that men and women believe in God because of their psychological need for a parent to guide and protect them through life. According to Freud, God exists only in the creative minds and imaginations of people hungering for the security of childhood.

Even though in the first round of my personal debate with Dr. Freud, I had to admit his rational argument made sense, his cold, analytic logic nevertheless frightened me. What if there were no God? What if a belief in God was a carry-over from a primitive era and the most widespread delusion of the modern age? Suddenly I identified with the characters in Samuel Beckett's play, *Waiting for Godot*— characters who huddle on a darkened stage waiting for a fabled character who never shows. I felt jilted and cosmically alone.

In my attempt to rally a defense for my belief in God, certain thoughts kept coming to me, and I tried to take comfort in them. Could my father and mother have been so deceived? Could their parents and their parents and generations of Christians before them have worshiped only a comforting illusion? I tried to convince myself that certainly not all of these people could have been wrong. But I found less and less comfort in the faith of my fathers. I knew that what really mattered was not what *they* believed, but what *I* believed. Freud had been reared on the faith of his fathers, and this genius had departed from the company of heredity and tradition and had chosen not to believe in God. I realized that the faith of my fathers could carry me to the threshold of adulthood, but no further. From then on, I was on my own to look at all the evidence and decide the fate of God for my own life. Freud rested his case. And it rested heavily on me.

For many weeks, the bearded specter of Freud haunted me. Though there were other matters that occupied me, my worries concerning the existence of God were never far from the surface of my consciousness. In moments late at night or whenever I found myself alone without distractions, these thoughts would rise up, and I would swallow hard, trying to push them down. They simply stuck in my throat, and I felt emotionally stifled and spiritually choked.

One day, while I was sitting in some now-forgotten class and gazing vacantly out a window, a simple but profound thought floated into my mind and suddenly filled my being: *Freud was a Jew, thinking like a Jew, and I am a Christian, thinking like a Christian. And there is a big difference in perspective.*

As simple as that thought sounds, it was the key that unlocked my theological paralysis and removed the wedged thoughts from my throat, allowing me at least to stammer out a refutation to Freud's devastating argument.

In that moment I realized that, as a Jew, Freud did not believe that God was revealed in Jesus Christ. Indeed, Freud thought Jesus Christ was a fake, a mistaken religious genius who overstepped his bounds. He did not believe that Jesus was living proof that God the Father was real or that the image of God the Father could be seen in the teaching and healing and resurrection of Jesus. For Freud, the testimony of Jesus Christ was inadmissible evidence in the trial for the existence of God, in which Freud was the prosecuting attorney. Jesus Christ could not be subpoenaed to give testimony or bear witness to the existence of God. Freud simply cross-examined an empty chair.

On the other hand, I, as a Christian, supposedly believed in God because "God was revealed in Jesus Christ." I believed because the transparent love of Jesus, the healing power of Jesus, the resurrection of Jesus all supposedly pointed to a power beyond and within Jesus that could only be called the Spirit of God.

Suddenly, I realized that the real issue at hand was not proving or disproving the existence of God.

Rather, the issue was whether Jesus was "right," whether Jesus was who he said he was, whether, in Jesus, God was truly seen. And I recognized that if Jesus were wrong, then Freud was right. Without the testimony of Jesus, the existence of God really was a moot question, impossible to prove either way. If Jesus was not raised by the power of God, then God is quite possibly only a mental projection, a fanciful childish hope in the minds of grown men and women.

As I turned my gaze from the window to the lecture at hand, I knew that, if I was ever going to have an adult faith in God, it would have to be because I had found just reason to believe in Jesus Christ. I had never before thought about God in this way. I had always thought that you first developed a belief in God, then worried about whether you believed in Jesus Christ. I had assumed that the existence of God was independent of the issue of Jesus. Now I had come to see that I must deal first with the credibility of Jesus and his testimony, and that only then could the existence of God become a living issue.

For me, the whole issue suddenly became simple: If Jesus was not right and his witness was not credible, then God did not exist. If Jesus was wrong, then Freud was right. For the first time, a twenty-year-old raised in a Southern Baptist church was dangerously close to becoming a Christian.

9

Escaping Decisions

As my junior year at Mercer progressed, I became gradually more comfortable and at ease in the company of Dr. Freud and his other colleagues in the field of psychology. I began to read the works of Carl Jung, Abraham Maslow, Erich Fromm, Viktor Frankl, Rollo May, and many other psychologists and psychiatrists. As each of these men held up his own unique mirror of self-examination before my face, I became a little less frightened at looking into my own eyes and peering into the darkness within me.

Even though my interest in psychology was increasing, I did not become any less interested in religion. I continued to take courses in biblical studies and theology and was intrigued by it all. I would have been quite content simply to continue taking random courses that interested me had not the dean's office officially informed me that I could not matriculate for another quarter without declaring an academic major. Unavoidably, the time had come to make some firm decisions. Would I major in psychology or religion?

Fearing decisions more than I feared the dean's office, I decided not to decide. I simply declared a double major in psychology and religion. Having barely escaped flunking out of school during my freshman and sophomore years, such an ambitious undertaking seemed to be ridiculous. But a strange thing was happening—my grades were improving. In the midst of taking courses that truly interested me, I had at last stumbled upon the secret of true academic success—self-motivation. I was finally becoming intellectually curious and challenged.

But my improving grades and my finally declared majors did not take away the nagging question of vocation. Graduation was not that far off. And what was I going to do with my life then? There was an urgent sense within me that my life must count for something important. I did not want just to form a life based on gaining comfort or security. I wanted to live *for* something.

More than anything, I hoped I could latch on to a cause or a purpose that was worthy of my total dedication. I found that the phrase "ultimate values" kept creeping into my conversations and onto the pages of a journal I was keeping for a literature class. I don't know where I learned the phrase, but it meant a great deal to me. It meant that I wanted to invest my life in something that was not an illusion nor a charade. As we used to say a lot in the early 1970s, I wanted something "real."

During this time, I became quite enamored with Miguel de Cervantes's novel, *Don Quixote de la Mancha.* The central character, Don Quixote, captured my imagination and symbolized something of great importance to me. Yet, reflecting on the character of Don Quixote stirred up conflict within me.

On the one hand, Don Quixote was obviously a demented and neurotic character who was totally out of touch with reality—an old fool in rusty armor, tilting at windmills. But on the other hand, he was a man who had a vision, a purpose, a passionate reason to live. He had a dream—even if it was an "impossible" one—and a quest that captivated his very being.

I wanted that kind of vision and purpose in my own life; I found myself singing "The Impossible Dream" with gusto. At the same time, however, I didn't want to be an old fool; I wanted to be a realist! I didn't want to give my life in the service of a kingdom or a cause that never existed in the first place. I wanted a dream in my life—yes, but not a delusion.

During the time that I was reading Cervantes for a literature class, I was also reading the works of some of the existentialist philosophers—Sartre, Camus, Nietzsche, and others. I admired the dogged realism of these men. They stared life in the eye and experienced the full range of emotions without flinching. Rather than retreating into fantasy, they held on to raw reality with bloodied fingernails. Yet, though I respected their courage, I also sensed that an overly zealous cynicism and a rigid rationalism which ruled out all quixotic quests and noble visions was also a distortion of reality. The truth lay somewhere between the fantasy world of Don Quixote and a cynical existentialism, and I was struggling to find this middle ground. I respected the existentialists. But I loved Don Quixote.

However, I still had no idea what I wanted to do when I walked off the stage, diploma in hand. I was beginning to feel the panic of a baby being thrust out of the sanctuary of the womb. And in many ways, school had been exactly that—a protective womb in which to grow and to receive preparation for life in the "real world." For sixteen of the twenty-two years of my life, I had been a student. I had learned that role well. But soon school would be over, and my identity and lifestyle would be in need of redirection. I needed to decide very soon on a vocation.

As luck would have it, however, I was soon rescued again from having to make an immediate decision. Two months before graduation, I was contacted by a friend, Jerry Jones, who worked for the Southern Baptist Foreign Mission Board. He offered me a very unique and appealing job opportunity.

Jerry's specific responsibility with the Foreign Mission Board was visiting college campuses across the United States and talking with interested students about the purpose and importance of foreign missions. More particularly, Jerry helped students become familiar with the Journeyman Program, a Baptist version of the Peace Corps, which gives college students an opportunity to spend two years in an overseas assignment assisting career missionaries. To aid in this task, Jerry was forming a "missions interpretation team" to travel with him and communicate to college students the significance and needs of foreign missions.

The team was to be composed of five young college graduates who had extensive experience in an overseas mission setting. In addition, the team members were to form a music group that could interpret the meaning of missions through concerts.

When Jerry asked me to be a part of the team, I asked him to let me think about it. And I did—for about thirty seconds. With great excitement, I accepted his offer and breathed a sigh of relief that at least for one more year I could put off the decision of whether I was going to attend graduate school or cook hamburgers at McDonald's. For one blessed year, I could travel, unwind from the pressures of school, and do what I knew I enjoyed most—relating to and communicating with people. College was coming to an end, and the world beckoned.

10

The Gamble

One of the first things that a new music group must do is to find a name. Our group called itself "Grain." Initially, we stole the idea from a cereal box. But the deeper meaning behind our choice of the word was derived from the Gospel of John, where the writer states, "Unless a grain of wheat falls into the earth and dies, it remains by itself alone; but if it dies, it bears much fruit" (12:24). Within six months, the meaning of this verse was to change my life.

The team members of Grain met for the first time at Meredith College in Raleigh, North Carolina, where we spent six weeks of intense practice before departing on our first concert tour. We were all vocalists, and it took some time to merge five voices into one harmonious sound. It required even longer to mesh five very different personalities into a closely knit group.

The "Grain family," as we called it, was composed of Jerry Jones, Steve Cheyne, Mary Kay Johnson, Nancy Crider, and myself. We each had experience in overseas settings. Jerry had been a Journeyman in Austria; Mary Kay had been a Journeyman in Vietnam; Nancy had spent time with her brother, who was a missionary in Spain; and Steve had been reared in Rhodesia and Ethiopia, where his parents were missionaries; and I, of course, had spent much of my childhood in the Philippines. Our combined backgrounds and experiences spanned the globe. Our purpose for being together was to share with others through personal testimony the physical and spiritual needs that we had seen in these very different corners of the world.

When the six weeks of initial practice was over and some semblance of a repertoire of music had been put together, we set off on our first four-month-long concert tour. We traveled in a dark blue Pontiac station wagon that we dubbed the "Grain Wagon." Crammed in amidst all our equipment—including six-foot-tall column speakers, an amplifier, microphone stands, and so on—we soon came to know each other very well.

Sitting elbow-to-elbow and catnapping on each other's shoulders for hours at a time, our group soon came to tear down interpersonal walls and to develop a real sense of intimacy. This does not mean that everything was all smiles. As in a marriage, we had to learn to share with each other the whole gamut of our emotions and personalities. But that was what made us truly intimate. We were forced to be ourselves, to be real.

We stayed at countless Holiday Inns, Best Westerns, Sheratons, and college dormitories. I honestly think we sampled the food from every chain restaurant that dots the highway system in America. Touring over thirty colleges in four months, we were a bunch of musical gypsies living in a car by day and singing by night. It was a very exciting, very good life. It was also very demanding and fatiguing.

Sitting in the Grain Wagon for long hours, I had much time to think and to read. Listening to hundreds of college students talk about their plans in life, their religious faith, and their own search for meaning also served as a great stimulus for my thoughts. During this time, I began to read the books of Leslie Weatherhead, Dag Hammarskjöld, and John Powell—men who also openly struggled for belief in God as well as faith in themselves. All this served as a very rich catalyst for personal reflection and growth.

But something was pricking at my conscience. I was no longer a college student inhabiting the ivory tower of theological questioning and skepticism. Now, I was a salaried representative of the Southern Baptist Foreign Mission Board. As such, I was daily finding myself on a stage, addressing hundreds of college students about the world's need to be brought into a relationship with God through faith in Jesus

Christ. Through word and song, I proclaimed this message with great confidence over and over again. And yet, inside, I knew that my intellectual battle for faith in Jesus Christ was still continuing.

On an emotional level, I was partially moored to the strong faith of my parents and their heritage, and I echoed its fervor. Intellectually, however, I was still looking for missing pieces of the puzzle of faith. Sometimes I felt as if I were straddling a fence, with one foot planted on the solid ground of faith and the other sinking in a quagmire of doubt.

The fact that I was publicly testifying to an evangelical faith with an air of confidence I didn't always feel did not seem blatantly dishonest, for a large part of me resonated with the faith of my fathers. But it did make me feel that I was telling half-truths. I felt spiritually incongruent, and this bothered me.

As we continued to travel together during the fall of 1973, I came across a book entitled *A Place to Stand*, by the great Quaker theologian and philosopher, Elton Trueblood. Within the pages of this book, I discovered a man who was intellectually credible and honest—who could express doubt—and yet who could develop analytically and with clarity a reasoned approach for his belief in Jesus Christ. Here was someone of open mind and sound reason who was able to get off the fence, to plant both feet on the ground of faith, and at the same time to tell me with clarity why he did so! I found myself carefully underlining passage after passage in Trueblood's book as the Grain Wagon rolled down the highways and the days merged into weeks.

After Grain had been on the road for several months, fatigue began to have its effect on us all. So we decided to take a couple of days off and stop at a friend's vacation cabin in the mountains of North Carolina. Secluded and surrounded by beauty, it was a great place to retreat from the world, to find rest and breathing room.

But even though I was sleeping late in the mornings, taking long walks, laughing freely, and catnapping at will, my mind was not slowing down. In fact, the solitude and the break in routine only sped up and intensified my nagging thoughts about my faith in Christ. Sitting by the warmth of the cabin's rock fireplace, I would mull over and over again many of Trueblood's thoughts and present my own lines of reasoning—assent or refutation. Though I had never met Trueblood, he was becoming a close and familiar companion.

Late one night near the end of our vacation time, I left the cabin and took a long walk alone. The air was cool and crisp and, in the dense darkness of the mountains, it seemed that every star in the sky was brighter and closer than ever before. I thought of my midnight reveries as a teenager, my backyard cathedral of the stars, and I looked up to see my old friend Orion.

As I walked slowly and reflected on my life, I knew that a decision was at hand. I realized that I had to get off the fence of uncertainty and plant both my feet on one side or the other. The time had come either to accept the testimony of Christ that he was the revealer of God or to reject that testimony and openly to say so.

As these thoughts pounded in my mind, one phrase from Trueblood's book kept returning over and over:

> At the deepest points of his life it is required of a man that he be a gambler, and in our greatest gamble it is reasonable to allow the testimony of Christ to tip the balance. A Christian is one who bets his life that Christ is right.[1]

As I pondered this thought, I sat down on a low rock wall that skirted the path. I knew that the time had come to wage my bet. All the childhood hours in Sunday school, the adolescent musings of the Marlboro Crew, the stimulating college courses in religion and psychology, and the mile after mile of pondering in the Grain Wagon—all these had come down to one point, one decision, a calculated gamble.

As I sat, I knew I didn't have all the answers I wanted to make this decision. There were still many unanswered questions concerning the nature of Jesus, the meaning of the cross, the validity of the resurrection, and even the existence of God. But I also sensed that I would never have the answers to all my questions, even if I lived for a thousand years.

In that moment, while sitting on a rock wall in North Carolina, I realized that the rational decision to believe in Jesus Christ could never be based on intellectual *certainty*, but only on a carefully analyzed *probability*. And deep in my soul, I knew where I believed the rational probability pointed. And, in a moment of time—a moment that spanned twenty-two years—I quietly placed my bet on the testimony of Christ. Both my feet touched the ground on the side of faith, and I began to walk home again.

11

Stalked

Having at last made the decision to accept the fact that Christ was the revealer of God and, thus, the Savior of the world, I began to feel some intellectual peace. Much of the storm of my theological struggle had been stilled by the act of commitment. However, even though the intellectual storm was dying down, there was brewing on the horizon another hurricane which, though interwoven with my Christian beliefs, was nonetheless separate from Christian commitment. This was an emotional struggle stemming from the rootlessness of my life. At twenty-two, I was feeling profoundly homeless in my world. And there was a very good reason for this feeling of homelessness.

As a six-year-old, I had been uprooted from familiar American soil and transplanted to the Philippines. As a child, I had not grown up within the security of an extended family—grandparents, uncles, aunts, and cousins. My relatives had always been on the other side of the world. They had sent us letters and packages, but I had not sat on their laps nor visited with them at Christmas time.

Then at age fourteen, I had been ripped up once again and returned to America, only to watch my father die and the cohesiveness of my immediate family unit die with him. I had again felt orphaned in a strange land and distant from family. To cope, I had learned to stay busy and "make it" in school.

But now I had graduated from the sanctuary of school into a world I did not know. No longer did I have fraternities, soccer teams, debate teams, choirs, and dorm life to give me the semblance of a feeling of belonging. I was living totally out of a suitcase, traveling from town to town, making friends on one day only to tell them good-bye the next. In other words, the lifestyle of Grain, though fun and exciting, nevertheless accentuated my feelings of rootlessness—feelings which were now bubbling up from the recesses of my subconscious world to the surface of my awareness.

As winter came upon the land and Thanksgiving merged into the first days of December, Grain moved from college to college across the bleak plains of west Texas. As I now reflect on those days, I have fleeting snapshot memories that reveal how emotionally vulnerable I was becoming. I recall particularly a groggy early morning moment when, lying in a motel bed, I tried in vain for a full minute to remember what town I was in. Finally, I had to roll over and look at the phone book on the bedside table to remember I was in Abilene. For me, the phone book symbolized exhaustion and disorientation.

There was also a quiet moment in a small snow-covered Texas panhandle town when, at dusk, I slipped quietly inside a church to meditate alone. I sat down on the back pew and blended into the recessed shadows. The sanctuary was dark when suddenly the choir loft was spotlighted, and choir members began gathering to rehearse Handel's *Messiah*. From the secreted shadows in which I sat, I could watch the rehearsal without being seen.

Anonymously, I looked at happy, windblown farmers' faces and the wholesome prairie smiles of young wives and several pretty girls. I listened to their folksy chatter and laughter as scores were distributed and felt the hush as all grew silent and the piano began to play. Then suddenly music filled the air—music like the Bethlehem shepherds must have heard. I had heard the *Messiah* sung many times by some of the best choirs in America, but never had I been so gripped by its passion and power as at this moment. At a different time in my life I would have noticed the out-of-tune piano, the nasal sounds of country altos, the strain of tenors reaching for notes that weren't quite there. But that night, I was overcome by sheer beauty, and I began to feel tears running down my cheeks. Burying my head in my arms on the pew before me, I began quietly to sob and shake in the darkness.

Somehow the music momentarily unleashed all the pent-up emotions inside of me—passion, grief, and loneliness. And I felt relief, as if a festered wound had been lanced. Yet, sitting in the shadows watching the choir through the prism of my tears, I had a sense that Handel's unleashing of my feelings was only a prelude of what was to come. I was more emotionally vulnerable than I had ever been before.

The rootless feelings of many years were relentlessly pressing toward the surface, and I was afraid of them. Not yet having the maturity to trust my emotions and welcome them as friends, I quaked at their presence. I feared an explosion, a big bang that would rend me apart and destroy me. And so I tried harder to ignore those feelings, to push them back below the surface. It could not be done.

12

A Crisis

A week before Christmas, we left the Grain Wagon in an airport parking lot and flew off to our respective homes in five different directions. As my plane hurtled down the runway and lifted into the air, I realized that I was glad to be on my way back to Georgia. I looked forward to going home. I wanted to slow down and stop traveling—to unpack my suitcase, stretch my legs, sit at my mother's table, and enjoy her good cooking. Best of all, a girl with whom I had been corresponding for several months—and with whom I was thoroughly infatuated—had agreed to come home with me to visit for a few days.

As I rode above the clouds, it seemed that I had transcended all traces of the nagging symptoms of grief and depression that had been creeping up on me. I could feel the warmth of the sunlight on my face as it radiated through the cabin window, and

I could see everything clearly for miles. It was good to be going home.

As the plane circled Atlanta, I realized that where I really wanted to go was to Fort Valley—back to the Marlboro Crew, the pecan trees in the backyard, and the Tastee-Freeze. I wanted to see my high school, to sit in the overstuffed chair by the window in my bedroom, and hug my old bulldog, Butch. But I knew this was not to be. Mom had recently moved to Atlanta to begin a new career. She had sold our house and closed another chapter in our life. Fort Valley was a place I could visit with fond remembrance, but it would never be "home" again.

Mom picked me up at the airport and drove me to her new condominium. Though the rooms were new, the furniture was familiar. All the Christmas ornaments from my childhood were displayed. And although they were in a different setting, they had a welcoming familiarity that brought a smile to my face. For the first time, it began to feel like Christmas.

Mom and I sat down and had coffee together and talked for a while alone. (My sister was not yet home from the University of Georgia.) And as we talked, I began to look at my mother with more than just my eyes; I tried to experience all over again what it was like to be mothered. I found that a part of me wanted to climb up on her lap again, to lean back into warmth, softness, and familiarity, to let her run her fingers through my hair as she had done when I was three. And yet there was another part of me that felt very distant. I felt as if I were talking to an old friend whom I hadn't seen in years, a child-hood companion lost in junior-high school. It had been five years since I had left to go to college, and once I had left, I had never really come home.

As Mom cooked supper and familiar aromas filled the house, I snuggled up under an afghan on the couch. I wanted to sleep for years—to rest behind a curtain of sleep, to lie like a cat in a bay window on a sunny day, to escape everything unpleasant and to stop feeling or thinking. I wanted to turn off and wake up refreshed and new. Fatigue had taken its toll.

After a nap and a delicious dinner, I decided to do some Christmas shopping. The next morning, I planned to drive to Birmingham to pick up my girl-friend, Dale, and bring her to Atlanta. As I mean-dered through a crowded mall and gazed in the bright store windows, I wondered what gift to buy for her. I wanted something nice—something with the warmth and softness of a sweater or a cuddly stuffed animal, something that reflected her personality and our relationship. But as I continued to look at win-dow displays, staring through my own reflection in the glass, I realized we hardly knew each other.

I had met Dale after a Grain concert three months before, and it had taken me two seconds to fall in love. She was tall, blonde, and a striking beauty! A nursing student, she had a gentle, caring nature that seemed to reach out and caress me. During the three months since our meeting, we had written let-ters and run up ridiculous phone bills, and I had spent many moments daydreaming about where our

91

relationship might lead. At Thanksgiving, we had rendezvoused in the mountain resort of Gatlinburg, Tennessee, and had spent two very infatuated days together. Now she was coming home to meet my family.

I couldn't wait to see Dale again. And yet, as I looked at an endless array of gifts, I was aware that my stomach was drawing into a knot. In spite of all those letters and phone calls and those idyllic two days in Gatlinburg, we simply had not had the time together to really know each other. And yet I was bringing her home for Christmas! I prayed she would still like me.

The next morning I drove to Birmingham. Sitting in the back seat hidden under my raincoat was the four-foot-tall Raggedy Ann doll that I had finally chosen for Dale. She collected Raggedy Ann paraphernalia, and I hoped she would like it.

While I was driving down the interstate highway, it began to drizzle, then to rain harder. As the windshield wipers pushed away the raindrops, I thought of all the days I had spent in the Philippines during my boyhood, whiling away the long drenched hours of the rainy season. As the rain pelted the windshield, I recalled our tin-roofed house and the typhoons that would whirl in from the South China Sea. Water would gush out of the sky for hours on end, and you could not hear a person talking in the next room over the din of giant raindrops banging on the roof like drumsticks on a snare drum.

I also remembered our crackling fireplace and the hours I spent in front of its warmth, evaporating the soggy days away by reading every Hardy Boys mystery book written. And when I was tired of reading, I would lose myself in battles with toy soldiers or in the marvelous pictures of *National Geographic* magazine.

There was time to take time then. There was a feeling of being at home when you were home. There was permission to lose yourself in mystery books, battlefields, and the jungles of Peru because you could always follow the string back home to reality again. I longed for those fireplace days. I did not want to retreat back to boyhood or the Philippines. But I wanted a fireplace again, a good book, and the soft blanketing presence of someone with whom to share it. I began to think of Dale.

As I stood in front of the elevator in Dale's dormitory watching the lighted numbers descend, my face felt tight. I practiced smiling, then quickly glanced around to make sure no one was watching what I knew must be a comical sight.

As I put my comb back into my pocket for the third time since parking the car, the doors slid open and there was Dale, smiling and beautiful. I don't think I breathed for a full ten minutes; with one long breath, I hugged her, talked a mile a minute, got her luggage in the car, and got the car back on the highway heading east. And when the next breath finally did come, I found I was holding her hand and probably breaking every knuckle, I was squeezing so hard. Gleefully, I told her to look under my raincoat in the back seat, and Raggedy Ann came to life. Dale loved her, and I felt the joy of giving a present that was just right. The kindling in the fireplace flickered, and the passing miles were lost in conversation.

Ten miles outside of Atlanta, however, the car grew a little quieter. Night had fallen. Raggedy Ann had gone to sleep. Questions had been asked and answers repeated, and I could tell Dale was growing tense as the reality and symbolism of entering my house and meeting my mother drew near. I began to feel anxious, too.

As we turned onto the perimeter highway that encircles Atlanta, I began to peer into the darkness for the exit leading to my mother's house, and everything suddenly looked unfamiliar. I had never before driven to Mother's home—my home—from this direction, and as the headlights flashed on the unfamiliar names of exit ramps, I began to feel a pervading sense of being lost.

Within me something very strange and unfamiliar was happening—something I would later learn to call an anxiety attack. I began to fight a growing sense of panic. A warm, electric sensation started shooting up my back and down my arms, and I began to grow light-headed, frightened as if a maniac were holding a gun against my head. As I gripped the steering wheel harder and tried to calm myself, I began to fear most of all that I was going to do something crazy and embarrass myself in front of Dale—something like crying or hyperventilating or jumping out of the car and desperately running away. My feelings seemed so bizarre, so inappropriate, so exaggerated, and so out of place that they scared me to death. I suddenly felt terrified of myself—which is the worst fear in the world.

Yet, on the outside, I must have appeared calm. Perhaps I seemed strangely quiet or preoccupied. But certainly I did not betray the absolute panic that was breaking loose within me. I sensed that the moment I had dreaded had come—the explosion was at hand; the dam walls were finally caving in. And yet, I had to drive a car, act self-assured, smile, and welcome Dale into a home that was not my home. I concentrated on breathing deeply and prayed that the right exit sign would soon appear. I wanted above all else to get out of the car and walk the panic away.

Mercifully, Mother's house was not far, and when I saw her exit sign flash in the darkness, I knew I would make it. The anxiety began to subside. But I felt so devastatingly weak, so childish and emotionally brittle. Here I was a grown man bringing a woman—my symbol of an adult world—home to meet my mother. And I was falling apart. Why? Why now of all times? Why, in a moment when my manhood was at stake and my ego so exposed, were things disintegrating? Why the panic and the fear? Why the longing for fireplaces and warmth and childhood? Why the growing fear of my own emotions?

With intense relief, I parked the car in Mother's garage and got out like a child rushing into daylight from a horror movie. I wanted to believe I had imagined the whole thing, that the five minutes of panic were only a nightmare. But as I lifted Dale's luggage from the trunk, I had to admit that it was all true.

95

And I prayed that it would never, ever, happen again. With a lightness and relaxed manner I did not feel, I brought Dale into the house and introduced her to my mother.

Mom had gone out of her way to prepare a delicious dinner for us. She had set the table with her fine china and silver, and I realized she was really enjoying the specialness of the moment. But even though I tried to act jovial and relaxed, I felt like a caged animal. I wanted to go outside and walk or run or do anything but sit still. I wanted to be alone. Yet a whole evening of being at home in the midst of quiet conversation loomed ahead, and once again I began to feel a surge of anxiety. As much as I tried to relax, I could not regain a sense of equilibrium. For the first time in my life, I sincerely wanted a tranquilizer or a shot of liquor—anything to calm me down.

After dinner and some time spent in talking with Mother, Dale and I went downstairs into the den to be alone. As we sat on the couch, I wanted to tell her how I was feeling—to hear her say she understood or had felt the same way before. But I couldn't bring myself to tell her. I didn't know how to talk about my feelings of the last few hours without sounding weak or neurotic or downright crazy. I wanted Dale to tell me I was OK. But I knew that in reality I was the only person who could do that. And I didn't *feel* OK; I felt less sure of myself than I had ever felt in my entire life. So, choosing not to talk, I turned on the stereo and, in the soft music, found an excuse for silence.

13

Crucified with Christ

The next morning, I awoke with a determination to start all over again and forget the terrible fears and feelings of the night before. I didn't think Dale had detected anything different about me; consequently, I decided to put that night behind me and get on with life.

However, as sleep began to wear off and I looked at my own eyes in the mirror while I was shaving, I began to feel a tinge of anxiety again. What if the panic recurred? What would happen if it sprang up stronger than before and I couldn't control it?

Suddenly I knew what my greatest fear was. I was afraid that I was on the brink of going out of control emotionally. The term *nervous breakdown* flickered through my mind, and I began to try to force myself to think about other things. Yet the thought kept coming back. What if I *were* having a nervous breakdown? What if things did get worse? What if I had to be hospitalized? I felt like slapping myself, telling myself to shut up and start thinking right, to snap out of it. But the thought had lodged immovably in my brain and I couldn't shake it. And though I didn't even know what a nervous breakdown was, my greatest fear was that I was dangerously close to having one. I had lost my self-confidence.

After a mid-morning breakfast, Dale and I rode around Atlanta and decided to browse in a large shopping mall. Walking hand-in-hand with her and talking animatedly, I was nevertheless preoccupied. And Dale wasn't fooled; she began to ask me what was wrong.

Over lunch and through the afternoon, I gradually began to talk. The words came first in a cautious trickle and then in a steady stream. I tried to describe my feelings without telling her everything. I admitted that I was uptight and that Christmas made me feel sad. But I could not tell her I was afraid of cracking up. I spoke of my rootless past, my father's death, and my struggle for faith, but I couldn't tell her that I feared the future. Though I could be partially open with her, I did not have the courage to say that at that moment I feared my own self and my own feelings. And yet, strangely, she seemed to understand.

As I talked, Dale began to share some of the struggles in her own life, and I knew that beneath the words we understood each other in a way that neither of us could verbalize. But I also began to feel that my struggle was kicking up some things inside

Dale that she didn't want to deal with, either. Though we were enjoying each other, we were also threatening each other. We were getting too deep too quickly. It was not a good time to be together.

The next day I drove Dale to Birmingham. We drove back around the perimeter of Atlanta and passed the same exit signs going in the opposite direction. Seeing the signs in the morning light brought back tremulous memories of the anxiety attack. But my fear level had lessened. Instead of anxiety, I was feeling depression. I was really down on myself because I sensed I had blown my relationship with Dale. I felt that a beautiful girl like Dale merited somebody strong and assured—a valiant knight on a prancing stallion. I once had felt that way. Now I felt like Don Quixote stripped of his delusions—a broken-down old man on a fleabag mule. My armor had been shattered. My dream was fading away. I was angry at life and furious with myself.

On the way to Birmingham, we talked a lot about things that I do not now recall. But at one point, Dale began to share with me how her Christian faith had brought her through some tough times. She said that the one verse of Scripture which had come to mean the most to her was from Paul's epistle to the Galatians:

I have been crucified with Christ; and it is no longer I who live, but Christ lives in me; and the life which I now live in the flesh I live by faith in the Son of God, who loved me, and delivered Himself up for me (Gal. 2:20).

When Dale quoted this verse, it sounded like something from Sunday school, rather trite and almost nonsensical. To me, it had the ring of a Zen koan such as "What is the sound of one hand clapping?"—something that is supposed to be spiritually profound but which defies analytic logic. I slid over the familiar surface of the verse as if it were ice. But later, when the rest of the conversation faded from memory, the verse stuck with me. In future days, I reflected on Dale's gift of Paul's words many times.

14

A Glint of Resurrection

Christmas Day came, and I found that unwrapping gaily decorated gifts did not lighten the depression I was feeling. This was a new experience for me. In the past I had had down moments, but never before had I been despondent. For the most part, I had always been characterized as outgoing and happy-go-lucky.

Now, I could not deny that depression was settling in. I was concerned only with escaping it. And I did not have the knowledge or the experiential maturity to see that my depression was really a friend— a friend banging frantically on my door in the middle of the night trying to awaken me and tell me my house was on fire.

Little did I know that deep within me were smoldering embers of anger and grief. I was angry with God for ripping away any sense of at-home-ness in my life. I was furious with my father for dying and leaving our family adrift. I was galled at myself for experiencing the humiliating emotions of anxiety and fear. And yet I was not consciously aware that I was angry at anything. I was emotionally asleep. And my depression was trying to arouse and alert me to the fact that the glowing embers were igniting into a blaze. Like a groggy man smelling smoke, my first reaction was to panic.

That was why I experienced the anxiety attack on the highway with Dale. For a lucid moment, I had "awakened" to realize I was lost and homeless—that my house was on fire—and I had panicked. Though I can see all this in retrospect, at the time I had no understanding of what was happening to me; there was only the irrational panic itself. And worst of all was the consuming fear that the anxiety and depression would steadily worsen until I lost all control and had a nervous breakdown—that phrase I had heard but never understood. I was caught in an emotional whirlpool.

I tried to talk to my mother. Though she was caring and openly concerned, it became clear that she did not understand my emotions any more than I did. And as for God, well, I spent much time praying desperately for release from fear and depression. But for the time being, God wasn't granting these wishes. Instead, he was mercifully allowing me to listen to the knocking of depression. He wanted me to wake up and attend to the destructive fires burning deep within me.

102

When my mother had no answers and when God did not give me the answers I wanted, I felt very much alone. I was isolated and cut off—a prisoner in solitary confinement.

The day after Christmas brought with it the realization that I would soon be returning to Grain. The thought made me cringe. Of all things, I did not want to go back to a lifestyle of traveling and rootlessness. At that moment, I wanted to pull into myself and risk no more exposure to pain. I did not want to stay in Atlanta. But I also did not want to jump into another five-month concert tour. I was in a difficult dilemma.

Finally, I decided that I could not return to Grain. What I felt I needed most was to consult a professional counselor or psychologist. Six months before, I—the psychology major—would have balked at this idea. Now I longed for someone else to help me understand myself and lend support. For eight years, I had gritted my teeth and gone it alone. But no more! I was now willing to seek a helping hand, a listening ear, a wiser counsel than I could offer myself.

Nervously picking up the telephone, I called my supervisor, Dr. Stan Nelson, and told him of my decision to resign. I did not expect his reaction. Though sympathetic, he firmly informed me that if I quit, the entire Grain project would have to be scrapped. There was not enough time to train another team member. At the very least, he felt I should fly to Richmond and talk with him face-to-face about my situation. Reluctantly and timidly, I agreed to do so.

After making reservations to fly to Richmond the very next day, I slipped on a warm-up suit and began jogging to while away the afternoon. For years I had enjoyed running. As a teenager, I had pounded away hundreds of miles getting in shape for football and tennis. During college I had continued this pattern. But now, as I ran down cold and foggy streets, I could not help thinking that running was a fitting symbol of my life.

When I finally tired, I stopped to find I was in front of a large cemetery. It had been beautifully landscaped like a park with rolling hills, walking paths, and picturesque ponds. Yet despite the landscaped beauty, a shroud of fog gave the cemetery a heightened aura of death.

Deciding to explore, I soon discovered a large hill in the cemetery. At the summit loomed a large marble cross with a life-sized figure of Jesus hanging upon it. Following an impulse, I climbed the hill and stood at the foot of the cross, gazing up at the stone-cold face.

For some reason, I began to try to put myself in Jesus' place. How would it have felt to be seized and beaten and tortured? I realized there could be no worse feeling of being out of control than to have your hands and feet nailed to planks and be hoisted naked for all the world to see. It suddenly struck me that Jesus must also have felt utter panic and fear and that he must have had to fight to suppress it. I could almost hear his blood-curdling scream: "My God! My God! Why have you forsaken me?"

I swallowed hard. And then Dale's words—Paul's words—came flooding back: "I have been crucified with Christ." Suddenly, the nonsensical cliche began to make sense. Deep in my soul, I somehow realized that until one is thrown out of personal control, until one is nailed down to one of life's many crosses, he or she can never have the opportunity to utter, in a spirit of weakness that is in reality strength, "Father, into thy hands I commit my spirit."

I could now in some measure identify with Jesus. For in a way I was undergoing my own death experience. My life had been seized and thrown out of control. I had been crucified with Christ. Like a whimpering child, I knew at a deep emotional level that more than anything I wanted to say, "Father, into thy hands I commit my spirit," and truly believe he would take care of me.

Turning, I walked down the other side of the hill and found at the base another sculptured scenario— this one of the resurrection. A cave was carved in the hillside with a large stone rolled to one side. Beside the stone stood a marble angel. Looking into the cavernous tomb, I thought of Jesus lying there for three days, his flesh rotting.

I thought of the deadness in me, the shroud of depression. I wondered if I would ever live again, if I could crawl out of the grave to new life. I didn't know. All I knew was that I had been crucified.

Yet, as I walked out of the cemetery and began

to run again, I could not help seeing through the fog a faint glimmer of hope. The age-old symbolism of the cross, the grave, and the resurrection had made a new and profound impression on me. I knew I was still in the grave. But now I began to hope for resurrection—a resurrection that could only be a gift from God.

15

Unwrapping
the Grave Clothes

Standing in front of Stan Nelson's office door, my knees trembled. How could I tell him all the things with which I was struggling? But if I did not tell him everything, then nothing would make sense. I loved and respected Stan; I had even placed him on somewhat of a pedestal. I wanted him to respect me, too. But I was afraid that if I told him about my past, my thoughts and my fears, he would indeed understand me, but no longer respect me. Indeed, returning to Grain might not even be an option. I half expected he would make me an appointment with a psychiatrist.

Four hours later, we were still talking in Stan's office. Much to my surprise, my words came easily. Once the pump was primed, then all my frightened, lonely feelings seemed to gush forward.

Stan listened. He listened intently. And it was

not long before I knew through his comments that, though his story was different from mine, he could relate to almost everything I said. Stan's quiet listening embraced me in a very loving way, and for the first time in years, I felt as if somebody had actually heard me and touched me—the real me. Now, at least one person in the world really knew Scott Walker.

Near the end of our conversation, much to my surprise, Stan suggested that I should not drop out of Grain and immediately enter counseling. Instead, he felt I needed to get back into the flow of life and not become too fixated on my problems. Though he did think that counseling was something I should eventually pursue, he let me know he did not think that I was crazy or unbalanced or sick. He saw me as a normal young adult coming face to face with some of the hardest realities of life—homelessness, grief, and repressed childhood emotions. He helped me see that for some adults these feelings gradually surface over time and are slowly confronted and assimilated. For other adults, such as myself, there are jagged crisis moments when events in life cause the repressed feelings suddenly to surge forward and be felt in a heightened and intense way. Regardless of the timing and the intensity of these experiences, most adults have to face up to the issues they represent. This was good news for me to hear. I felt less lonely and strange.

I spent that night with Stan and his wife, Norma. After an evening of quiet conversation and playing chess, I curled up on a pallet in front of their fireplace and began to drift off into sleep. The fire was dying down, the embers were glowing brightly, and my whole body felt warmed. My thoughts went back to our fireplace in the Philippines, and I began to feel at home for the first time in years. Somehow the talking, the divulging of secrets, had begun to unleash a resurrection experience within me—it was almost like coming back from the dead. I began to think of returning to my Grain family.

As I lay by the hearth, the word *grain* pounded through my mind, and I began to recite quietly the familiar words of Jesus: "Truly, truly, I say to you, unless a grain of wheat falls into the earth and dies, it remains by itself alone; but if it dies, it bears much fruit." Suddenly, *Grain* was more to me than a clever name for a religious singing group. Now the theological significance of the word had deep personal meaning as well. I now knew that in order to escape the prison of my loneliness and to be fruitful, I—the grain—had first to be buried and to die in order eventually to sprout forth and spring up into new life.

The anxiety and depression of the past weeks had been the death throes of a dying man. Death had come. The hope of new life was now drawing near. Curled up before the crackling hearth of God, a prodigal had once again come limping home.

16

Healing

It was good to see the members of Grain again. They really did seem like family—my brothers and sisters. It was difficult to tell them about the events of the three-week Christmas break, but they were willing to listen and provide support. Once back with the group, I realized how great a mistake it would have been to stay at my mother's and isolate myself while I fixated on my own struggle. I needed my Grain family; they were in a real sense my church, my group of fellow travelers. And they needed me, too.

It was also good to sing again. It felt so liberating to pick up a microphone, sense the mood of an audience, and fling myself into a song with all the expression I could muster.

I also noticed that I now had far more sensitivity than ever before in talking and listening to college students. When a student told me he was depressed or anxious or struggling, I no longer responded like a psychology major with a head full of book knowledge. I now listened with the understanding and the compassion of one who had walked a similar road.

In a sense, my struggle was increasingly humanizing me, making me into a gentler, more open person. I began to realize that the most loving thing I could do for another person was to allow him truly to get to know me, "warts and all." When this type of openness transpired between us, I suddenly found a sense of unity I had previously missed. I began to break out of my somewhat morbid introspective shell and to reach out to others.

Over the course of the next few weeks, Dale and I decided that for many reasons our friendship should not continue to grow in a romantic way. We truly cared for each other, but distance and timing and our overall personalities and needs did not point toward a more serious relationship. There was mutual hurt involved in this decision, but we each sensed it was right. I will always be thankful, however, for the support and the testimony of this beautiful girl during a crucial time in my life.

It is often true, however, that when romance begins to dim beyond the western horizon, it reappears as a new sunrise in the east. For me, this was certainly true. I well remember when this new light began to glimmer.

It was still winter, and Grain had driven nonstop from Oklahoma City to Louisville, Kentucky, to

perform at a missions conference for college students
sponsored by the Southern Baptist Theological Seminary. Arriving in the afternoon, we had wearily flung
ourselves into bed to gain a few hours sleep before
the evening concert. Having hit the snooze button
on the alarm clock too many times, I awoke twenty
minutes before the concert was to begin. I threw
on my clothes and was running across the seminary
campus through a light blowing snow when I suddenly collided with a girl walking toward the audi-
torium. Stopping to apologize, I looked into her
eyes and gasped. It was Beth Rushton, the most
beautiful girl I had known during college days in
Georgia.

Though Beth and I had attended different colleges,
we had seen each other twice a year at Baptist Student Union conventions. And I had always made
a point of speaking to her—but so had a hundred
other guys! When I occasionally visited her campus
for a debate tournament, I had called her. I remember
telling my roommate once that if I had to choose
a girl to marry at that moment, I would choose Beth.
Besides her beauty, she had a quiet, unpretentious
softness that captivated me. But for some reason she
had also intimidated me. Rather than risk rejection,
I simply had never asked her out.

But now, in the middle of a Kentucky snowstorm,
I found myself throwing my arms around this girl
from Georgia. Before I regained my senses, I blurted
out that I would like to see her after the performance
and ran on. All during the concert, I looked for her,

and finally I saw her sitting in the balcony with another fellow. My heart sank. But after the concert she did come up to the stage, and we left to get a cup of coffee and talk.

Over the course of the next two days, Beth and I spent a lot of time together. I could tell I was quickly becoming infatuated, but after the emotional fiasco of Christmas and the breakup with Dale, I was not sure I wanted to risk getting involved in another vulnerable relationship. Yet every time I looked into Beth's blue eyes, the risk factor melted a little more. We agreed to write each other and stay in contact during the weeks ahead. Grain was contracted to stay together four more months and then disband. And so, for the remainder of this time, Beth and I wrote long letters and supported Southern Bell.

As the weeks flew by and the conclusion of the Grain experience began to stare me in the face, I once again was faced with a vocational decision. What did I want to do with my life?

As I thought and prayed about this matter, I realized I was beginning to discern a sense of direction developing I could not have visualized as a college senior. More and more, I was feeling the desire to commit my life to some form of Christian ministry. Granted, I still resisted entering the ecclesiastical barn. I still chafed at the stereotypical "preacher" mold. But, having made a rational and experiential commitment to Christ during recent months, I realized in a deeper sense that I was being truly called

113

into the ministry and that, furthermore, I yearned to follow that calling!

How did I feel "called"? There were no voices nor lights nor street signs that said "go." But there was a continuing realization that I wanted to give my life to the only ultimate cause I knew—Christianity. And furthermore, all the skills and talents I had been developing over a lifetime—debate, drama, music, the love of people—were all pointing me toward some form of professional ministry.

At that time, I was quite certain that I did not want to be a minister in a local church. But the thought of being a minister to college students or a religion professor or a Christian social worker was appealing. So, guided by this thinking, I decided to apply to the Southern Baptist Theological Seminary in Louisville. I reasoned that if I didn't like it, I could always leave.

I also decided to move to Louisville a few months before seminary classes started in the fall and to begin the counseling process I was both hungering for and dreading. I knew of a very renowned pastoral counselor, Dr. Wayne Oates, who taught at the Southern Baptist Theological Seminary, and I determined to try to establish a counseling relationship with him.

In short, after the life-wrenching storm during the previous months, things were beginning to fall into place. A sense of direction was emerging in my life, and an opportunity to "get my house in order" through counseling was becoming available. I began to sense that God was truly working through all things—the good, the bad, and the ugly—to bring wholeness into my life. I was also learning that God always provides a way to supply all our needs at the proper time. I was beginning to feel the reality of rebirth, of resurrection.

17

"He Will Reveal Himself"

When Grain disbanded in May of 1974, there was a lot of sweet sorrow. Jerry, Mary Kay, Nancy, Roger, and Stan Nelson were perhaps the closest friends I had ever known. We had truly grown to love each other and separation was painful. But in that depth of love was a realization that our commitment to each other would remain. (Years later, this has proven to be true.)

But as Grain dissolved and I flew back to Georgia, I felt both relief and excitement—relief that the constant travel was over and that Grain had been such a success, excitement and anticipation for what lay in store.

There was one situation awaiting me at home that I didn't quite know how to handle—but I certainly liked! During Beth's last quarter in college, she had been requested to complete an internship in social work and had been accepted to an internship in Atlanta. Then she had been faced with the problem of moving to the big city. With tongue in cheek, I had suggested one night during a phone conversation that she should see whether a basement apartment my mother sometimes rented was available. Much to my surprise, she had done exactly that. Now as I was returning to Atlanta, I was faced with the fact that Beth was actually living in my old bedroom. It was a strange situation, but it did make it possible for us to spend a lot of time together.

In the course of the four weeks that I was in Atlanta before moving to the seminary, Beth and I grew closer and closer. A good friendship began to take on the characteristics of a definite romance. And when the time came for me to move to Louisville, I was quite reluctant to go.

But move I did. Loading everything I owned into my old green Oldsmobile, I sadly told Beth goodbye, hoping against hope that the distance would not dissolve our relationship. But as I drove north toward Louisville, I began to feel excited as well as sad. I sensed that a new chapter in my life was opening.

The first thing that I did upon arriving in Louisville was to call Dr. Oates about establishing a counseling relationship. Fortunately, he had some time available and agreed to meet with me once a week for a three-month period. The second thing I did was to get a job as a house painter—a far cry from the old concert tour. The third, and most important, thing I did was to make a plane reservation to fly back to Atlanta in two weeks. I was beginning to sense that I truly loved Beth, and I was determined that I was not going to let my relationship with her waver.

Over the course of the summer, Wayne Oates helped me see myself in a new perspective—perhaps God's perspective. He helped me not only to understand myself and the dynamics within me, but also to see myself through more compassionate and self-accepting eyes. I began to like myself again. Indeed, I began to see that, given the total story of my life, I had done reasonably well. Granted, I had made many mistakes, and I had to live with those. But overall, a feeling of self-respect and self-confidence was returning.

However, had I not been forced by pain to talk with people like Stan Nelson and Wayne Oates, the future of my life could have gone in a far less positive direction. Emotional pain channeled through the grace of God had resulted not in destruction but in healing. And the joints of my life became stronger than ever before.

By September, Beth and I became engaged, and in December we were married. Neither of us is the kind of person that characteristically rushes into things; but between phone calls, plane tickets, and stamps, we couldn't afford *not* to get married! In one short year, I had moved from one extreme to the other—from feeling the greatest loneliness in my life to experiencing the greatest joy of unity. It was hard to believe. But it was proof once again that God does truly provide for our needs.

As Beth and I were married and settled into our

118

first small furnished apartment, I became increasingly enthralled by and caught up in my seminary classes. I found I was particularly enjoying New Testament studies. I quickly discovered, however, that seminary was no Vacation Bible School experience. The course work was difficult, and the teachers forced me to think through my entire belief structure.

I found myself once again analyzing and questioning many things. But the resurrection experience I had recently gone through and commitments I had made gave me the courage to doubt and question. I still clung to the prayer I had uttered as a freshman at Furman: "Father, give me the faith that I will find faith," and I believed firmly that God would provide support for my faith. My task was to remain open-minded, inquisitive, and motivated to learn. I now knew that God was bigger than any of my questions. But I needed the experience of questioning and the struggle of finding faith in order to be a minister who could truly help others find their way. I needed to travel that rocky road first—the same road of doubt, self-questioning, and perseverance that Jesus trod.

Returning home from the seminary library late one night, I had an experience that I would like to recount as a fitting conclusion to this autobiographical study. In the process of studying the life of Jesus, it was required that I read *The Quest of the Historical Jesus,* the classic work of Dr. Albert Schweitzer. Schweitzer had always been one of my true heroes. Here was a man who at the turn of this century had given up worldwide acclaim as a theologian and a musician to go as a medical missionary to primitive Africa. I had always admired his compassion, single-minded commitment, and courage, but I had never read any of his theological works. Upon laboriously working my way through *The Quest of the Historical Jesus*, I came to realize how radical—and indeed unacceptable—some of Schweitzer's ideas were to me. As one of his true fans, I was disturbed by this discovery.

Late one night, I closed his book in the seminary library and drove home mulling through Schweitzer's thoughts. I felt confused and disturbed. I could not link the Schweitzer of simple faith and commitment with the Schweitzer of liberal—even radical—theology. Climbing up the steps to our apartment, I determined that I would read the final chapter of the book before going to bed.

Plopping down in my easy chair, I began to read. By the time I came to the last page, I was yawning. But the final paragraph of the book shook me wide awake—burning its imprint permanently on my mind. In his conclusive statement regarding his own searching to discover Jesus, Schweitzer had simply and poetically written:

He comes to us as One unknown, without a name, as of old, by the lakeside, He came to those men who knew Him not. He speaks to us the same word: "Follow thou me!" and sets us to the tasks which He has to fulfill for our time. He commands. And to those who obey Him, whether they be wise or

simple, He will reveal Himself in the toils, the conflicts, the sufferings which they shall pass through
in His fellowship, and, as an ineffable mystery, they
shall learn in their own experience Who He is.[1]

I was suddenly wide awake because what Schweitzer had written resonated with my deepest feelings.
Christ *does* walk down the shoreline of each of our
lives, and he comes to us as an unknown. Others
can tell us who he is, but this does not adequately
enable us to truly know him. Rather, we must all,
in our own way, discover who he is. And as Schweitzer so aptly perceived, we discover Christ only when
he reveals himself to us through the toils, the conflicts, and the sufferings of a lifetime. It requires a
lot of deaths and resurrections. It demands years
of following.

I turned off the lamp and sat in the darkness. I
knew that I didn't have all the answers—but neither
did Schweitzer nor Martin Luther nor the apostle
Paul. I knew my faith was often brittle and tenuous.
But one thing that I knew I could do was simply
to follow. I could put one foot in front of the other
each day of my life. That was all that Christ asked
me to do. And ahead lay a lifetime of discovery.

II

WHERE THE RIVERS FLOW

18

Introduction

In the first section of this book, I described my own process of developing faith over a twenty-five-year period. In essence, I charted a portion of the course of the river of my life. I did not, however, attempt to stop the river's flow nor artificially dam up the water to analyze its content. Rather, I related a free-flowing story with the emphasis upon the events that affected the development of my faith.

Now, however, the river has been charted. And the proper time has come to look back over its course. As we do so, I would encourage you to reflect on your life as well. What are the major components in my life—in your life—that lent themselves to the evolution of faith? What are the various elements that, when combined, result in belief and commitment? Though there are perhaps many, I have observed nine major contributing factors in the process of religious—and, in particular, Christian—faith development.

In presenting these factors, however, I am not attempting to construct a *system* of understanding. In other words, this is not a comprehensive systematic theology nor a wholistic approach to faith development. Rather, I present only some jagged fragments or pieces of understanding I have picked up on the riverbank as the current of life has carried me along. If you put the fragments together, they would not begin to comprise the whole of truth concerning faith development. But fragments, nonetheless, are better than nothing at all. Like an archaeologist who must rely on scattered shards of pottery to tell him of an entire civilization, I am well aware that there are many pieces missing. But the fragments, though limited, are infinitely precious to me. I hope they will be of value to you as well.

As I write these words, I am reminded of the apostle Paul, who spent a lifetime attempting to understand better the mystery of God and plumb the depths of the Christian faith. He, too, found that in the end he held only fragmentary knowledge. But the fragments were enough to allow him to write, in a spirit of hope and optimism, "For now we see in a mirror dimly, but then face to face; now I know in part, but then I shall know fully just as I also have been fully known" (1 Cor. 13:12).

I share this hope. And I share with joy what limited insight I have into the shadow that looms in the reflection of the dim mirror—the shadow of God.

19

Four Rivers of Universal Faith

I often think of the reservoir of religious faith within me as a deep and vibrant natural lake which is perpetually fed by four mighty rivers. Each of these contributing rivers contains a water whose composition is unique and which flows from a distinctly different source. The names of these rivers are *tradition*, *intuition*, *reason*, and *emotion*. These four rivers contribute to the faith of people of all religions throughout our world. In order to better understand the nature of faith, it is helpful first to study separately the nature and composition of each of these rivers.

THE RIVER OF TRADITION

All of us are born into this world through the union of two parents who have already largely developed their own religious thoughts, conceptions, practices, and biases before we are born. Their beliefs—and the beliefs of generations before them—form a *tradition* that as children we are prone to accept without question. Certainly, we reason, if Daddy and Mother believe a certain way, then what they think must be true. Our faith is initially the mirror image of our parents' faith.

Likewise, all of us are born into a society and a culture that shapes our traditional religious beliefs. In America, children put in their piggy banks coins which read, "In God We Trust." In the Soviet Union, the official dogma is atheism. In Boston, a young girl of Irish-Catholic descent goes to Mass at eight o'clock on Sunday mornings and attends a parochial school. In Georgia, a boy of English-Protestant descent attends Sunday worship services at eleven o'clock and goes to a public school. And, in Chicago, a girl of German descent has never seen the inside of a church, cathedral, or synagogue. The culture and locale into which we are born greatly influence the tradition of faith that we as children accept.

As the river of tradition winds its way toward the lake of faith, however, the water becomes turbulent and increasingly treacherous. This is due to the fact that, as children reach the developmental stage where they no longer blindly accept the tradition into which they have been born, they begin to appraise it critically. This critical assessment can happen during any stage of life.

For me, the first moment of questioning came when I began to doubt the reality of Santa Claus, a quasi-religious belief that the children of my culture hold dear. Later, as a teenager, I questioned what refraining from the fun of dancing had to do with, first, being a Baptist and, second, being a Christian.

We absorb traditional religious beliefs (or the lack of them) just as surely as we assimilate the language and practices of our culture. And sooner or later we also come to a point where, in our own way, we subpoena these traditional beliefs to trial, cross-examine them, and yield our own verdicts. This critical assessment continues through the various stages of life.

Now, the biggest issue of traditional faith, as I perceive it, is not so much whether its tenets are right or wrong, but rather whether or not we have taken the pains to think through our parents' faith carefully and decide for ourselves which of these tenets we will accept, reject, or modify. Often, we will find in this cross-examining process that in many of our decisions we totally agree with our parents, our pastor, our friends, and our culture. At other points, however, we may choose to modify certain attitudes and ideas or to disagree with them altogether. A term for this process of developing our own stance of faith over against the faith of tradition is the *integration of faith.*

Recently, I heard a man say, "When everyone is thinking alike, then no one is thinking." I believe there is much truth in this statement. When traditional faith is blindly followed and never appraised, then it is not *your* faith, but merely the faith of your fathers. It is not a faith that is truly woven and integrated into the total fabric of your being. Left unquestioned, it is probably not a faith that can stand up to the demands of a lifetime. In the words of Jesus, it is a house built upon sand.

A term that is often used for a traditional faith that is nonintegrated is *projected faith.* As I have grown to understand this term, I have often explained its meaning by referring to the difference between a photographic slide and an oil painting.

A faith that is based primarily on the blind acceptance of traditional beliefs is like the picture projected by a slide projector. The projector represents the parents or the culture who are projecting the picture of their faith onto their children, who serve as the reflective screen. As long as the parents are present to project the picture, then the children reflect their faith. But when the slide projector becomes unplugged or the screen is moved into another room, then the screen becomes blank. In essence, the picture of faith was never part of the screen. It was never real—only a projection. When I went to Furman University and enrolled in my first religion course, I soon discovered that much of my faith was projection.

In contrast, when an artist paints upon a canvas, the paint and brush strokes remain on the canvas regardless of whether the artist is present or absent. An integrated faith is one wherein the child, the teenager, or the adult critically looks at the blank canvas of his life. He then decides for himself the picture of faith he will create, the brush strokes he will use, the colors he will choose, and the perspective from which he will paint. The artist may choose to copy almost identically the picture that has been painted on the canvas of his parents' or his friends' lives. But even then he must take the brush in his own hand and go through the creative process of copying that picture, stroke by stroke, on his own canvas. The faith of tradition must be integrated over time and painted during many seasons if the picture is to remain when faith is challenged.

Jesus was an individual who was not afraid to question the faith of his fathers. He did not have a projected faith. Indeed, he rejected many of the Jewish laws which reflected more of the spirit of culture than the spirit of God. For instance, he ignored the Jewish laws that prohibited a righteous man from walking and talking with sinners. He turned the traditionalists—the Pharisees—on their orthodox ears by his individual interpretation of the Law. Jesus was a person who obviously spent much time appraising the Jewish tradition and developing his own integrated faith structure. He is a model whom we need not fear to follow.

But let me hasten to say also that there is much that is good and positive concerning the faith of tradition. The strength of traditional faith, as I see it, is that, once I have gone through the process of integration, then I can find a great assurance and strength in knowing that many of my beliefs are buttressed and supported by the best minds and spirits of generation after generation.

For instance, my father and I would probably

disagree on exactly how God created the world. Despite our differences of opinion, however, we would steadfastly agree that God created all things. And certainly we would agree that this God of Creation was one day revealed through the life of Jesus Christ.

Though our beliefs admittedly would differ at points, my father and my grandfather and my great-grandfather have all in our own way come to affirm the existence of God, the creative nature of God, and the revelatory nature of God through Jesus Christ. And in such a tradition of faith there is great strength, hope, assurance, and vitality.

THE RIVER OF INTUITION

There was a time, however, when there was no tradition of faith. The human race was young. There were no entrenched tribal customs, formal religions, earth-hewn temples, or written codes of Scripture. Rather, men and women stood new and naked before the universe and, holding their children in their arms, sensed in their deepest being that there was something that created them, something that parented and sustained them, something that gave rhythmic order to all of life. They experienced these intense primal feelings long before their primitive tongues could form the words to verbalize their emotions. And when at last their tongues did unleash their pent-up comprehension, they shouted and chanted and sang in thousands of languages and dialects that this Ultimate Being, this Cosmic Creator, this Force within the universe was "God."

132

But lest we assume that this innate comprehension of God is more characteristic of primitive than of modern man, we should look closely at our own contemporaries. In a recent nationwide survey conducted by the Gallup Poll, it was found that 93 percent of Americans professed some form of belief in God or a deistic force.[1] There is also strong evidence to point to the fact that this preponderance of a belief in God is true in other areas of the world as well. Thus, an almost universal comprehension of God remains a strong fiber within the thread that is woven into the basic fabric of men and women.

What is it that has caused human beings throughout the ages to sense that there is a God? Perhaps it is an automatic reflex or a religious instinct. Perhaps it is a "gut feeling." However, the word that best expresses for me this comprehending ability is *intuition.* Men and women have forever *intuited* the fact that there is a God.

But is intuitive perception—as some have maintained—only the remnant of primitive superstition? Or is there within us a legitimate capacity to perceive the essence of spiritual truth, which our five traditional senses cannot comprehend?

When, as a teenager, I walked under the cathedral of the stars in my backyard in rural Georgia and looked up into the night sky, I am convinced I saw far more than a void of black nothingness and the staccato shimmer of distant celestial bodies. Something behind my eyes also saw or intuited the shadow of God stretched across the universe.

Perhaps this "something behind my eyes" can best

be explained by using an analogy of the human eye and its capacity for vision. By their very construction, the human eye and the brain cooperate to form visual pictures of external objects. The eye acts as the body's "antenna" to pick up visual images and transmit these images via nerves to the brain. The other four senses—touch, smell, taste, and hearing—work in a similar way.

Now, everything that the human eye captures is encased by three dimensions—height, depth, and width. Although theoretically it is possible for an object to be so narrow that it has no width or so compressed that it has no height, such an idea is almost incomprehensible except as an intellectual exercise. Our eyes are limited to perceiving the three familiar dimensions of the visible world.

But what if there are other dimensions in addition to height, depth, and width—dimensions our human eyes and other sensory organs do not have the capability to discern? What if these other dimensions, like radio waves, constantly but invisibly surround us but cannot be comprehended without a "receiver"? What if there are elements of reality all about us that cannot be perceived through our five senses? Does this mean these other-dimensional realities do not exist? Not at all.

Now, let us pose another question. What if we *do* have a "receiver" to pick up the realities we cannot see, hear, touch, smell, or taste? What if there is within the human body of flesh and fluid and electrochemical interplay a sixth sense—a sense called intuition—that does not have a visible "antenna" such as an eye but that like an eye is capable of picking up signals and transmitting them to the brain. Perhaps it is this sixth sense—recessed among the undiscovered intricacies of the human brain— that perceives other-dimensional realities. Perhaps this is the eye behind the eye that sees the shadow of God when our retinas reflect only stars.

Could it really be that there are "dimensions" to life other than those our five senses perceive? I believe so. And I believe that one of these realities which we intuit but cannot see is the living presence of God which is all around us.

And so into the lake of faith flows the mystical river of intuition. It makes a contribution all its own. Here we find neither the mineral wealth of tradition nor the rich sediment of reason. Yet the waters of intuition sparkle with the primitive and spontaneous qualities of life. The river of intuition flickers back the sunlight on its surface and flows gleaming into the depths of the reservoir of faith.

THE RIVER OF REASON

Through the centuries, as men and women have been born into religious traditions and have intuitively sensed the shadow of God fall across their path, they have usually not been satisfied to simply *feel* God in a mystical, ambiguous way. They have also hungered to understand God intellectually and to prove his existence rationally. In effect, human beings have always wanted to place the waters from the rivers of tradition and intuition into a test tube and—through analysis, verification, logic, and philosophic probability—to capture God behind glass where he could be empirically observed.

But the essence of God has always escaped man's rational grasp; he is far too vast to be confined to a test tube. Perhaps Leslie Weatherhead, in his book, *The Christian Agnostic*, best expressed the frustration that comes from trying to rationally capture God:

> There is something almost ludicrous about sitting down at a desk and writing the word "God" at the top of a sheet of foolscap paper and then being presumptuous enough to add anything else.[2]

Even the famed theologian, Emil Brunner, who spent a lifetime trying to "systematize" a reasoned approach to belief in God, stated emphatically:

> The better we know God, the more we know and feel that His mystery is unfathomable. The doctrine which lays the most stress upon the mystery of God will be nearest to the truth.[3]

Thus, God cannot be proved, analyzed, or captured. We can see his shadow, but we cannot glimpse his face. Or, as Brunner also said, "God is mystery dwelling in the depths of 'inaccessible light.'"[4]

Nonetheless, the human intellect cries out to comprehend God rationally, and this cry cannot be stifled nor denied. In our scientific age, sensitive men and women may agree that God cannot be captured in a test tube, but they will simultaneously demand a faith that is at least rationally cogent. A faith that does not attempt to draw the shifting edges of God's shadow into a clearer intellectual focus is a faith which cannot be sold, traded, nor given away in the marketplace of modern times.

Sensing this truism, Elton Trueblood wrote in his book, *A Place to Stand:*

> Accordingly, one of the most urgent tasks of contemporary Christians is to express a faith which can be made credible for modern man. Enthusiasm is not enough! . . . No faith can survive unless it meets the double test of intellectual validity and social relevance. Few tasks are more important for Christians now than that of a reconsideration of the function of reason. We need to try to understand what reason can do and what it cannot. . . . Though reason alone may not enable men to find God, it can do wonders in enabling them to surmount serious barriers to the achievement of an examined faith.[5]

Thus, if a man or woman expects to come to a stance of mature faith, and to share that faith in the modern world, the river of reason must be allowed to empty into and contribute to the lake of faith.

When I encountered Sigmund Freud in my college psychology textbooks, I came face to face with an intellectual giant. When Freud informed me that God was only a psychic projection based on infantile need, my faith was greatly shaken. It was shaken because I had not taken the time—nor been faced by the need—to develop a foundation of faith that included the crafted stone of reason. When the storms of intellectual doubt came, my house of faith was found to be constructed on sand. As the sand began to shift and the house tilted perilously, I decided right then to begin to place some carefully selected ballast stones of reason within the foundation of my intellectual being. I have never regretted that decision. True, reason has often caused me to doubt. Yet I have come to see that there can be no faith without doubt. Indeed, doubt is an indispensable catalyst required for the process of faith to transpire. For the very word *faith* (as opposed to *knowledge*) presupposes doubt.

Thus, as we gaze upon the lake of faith, we find that the river of reason makes an invaluable contribution to its waters. True, when the mountain stream of reason cascades into the basin of faith, the calm surface of belief often becomes turbulent and even treacherous. But without the encounter with such churning water, the waters of the lake of faith can become placid, if not stagnant and lifeless.

THE RIVER OF EMOTION

There is at least one more contributing river that flows into the lake of universal religious faith—the river of *emotion*. I believe that one of the major contributions the field of psychology has made to the understanding of human nature is the realization that men and women are emotional beings. For too long it had been posited that if a person could only understand a problem, he or she could deal with it. But the reality is that a simple, rational understanding is not enough. Rather, one's emotions and feelings must be acknowledged and drawn forth if one is successfully to untangle personal problems and fully and healthily to engage in life. True, it is our high level of intelligence and reason that separates us from the animals. But it is our wide range of raw emotions that connects us to the earth, that makes us a kindred part of living things, and that makes us feel alive. We cannot ignore our emotions and be complete human beings—creatures made in the image of God.

Because of our emotional nature, our religious faith must also be firmly attached and rooted in our emotional experiences. This is glaringly evident in the story of my own life. For years, I ran from many of my emotions trying to suppress them—particularly the painful and negative emotions of fear, grief, displacement, and uprootedness. But it was only when my festering emotions boiled to the surface and forced me to engage in them—when I had to cry instead of think, groan instead of pray, feel instead of read, and be temporarily stuck in the doldrums of depression—that my faith in God came truly "alive." It was only in that very low moment in my life when emotions were raw and jagged and inescapable that I could for once understand what the great English pastor, James S. Stewart, had meant when he said:

It is when you have sunk right down to rock bottom that you suddenly find you have struck the Rock

139

of Ages. And then men begin to take knowledge of you that you have been with Jesus.[6]

Later, I learned to experience a full range of other emotions when, like Lazarus, I crawled out of a grave into new life. I learned to laugh, to rejoice, to experience praise and thanksgiving, to dance and to sing. And all of this vast panorama of emotions carried me closer to the presence of God than reason alone, or tradition alone, or intuition alone ever could.

The river of emotion is a buoyant water. It carries you along in its intense grasp and will not allow you to sink beneath the surface for long. It is alive. It is real. It vitalizes, refreshes, and cleanses the lake of faith. It filters impurities and keeps faith honest and strong and congruent with our true selves.

CONCLUSIONS

As I have gazed upon the waters of the four major rivers that lead to universal religious faith, I have been led to six basic conclusions. Each, though separate, is closely interrelated with the others.

(1) *Universal religious faith is derived from four major sources: tradition, intuition, reason, and emotion.* Without any one of these four components, faith cannot healthily exist for long. They are all vital and indispensable in the evolution of a belief structure.

(2) *These four "tributaries of faith" are of varying strengths and volumes in the life of each individual.* For instance, I may be by nature more

rationally oriented than you are. Therefore, the river of reason will contribute more to my faith structure than to yours. At the same time, you may be far more sensitive to and guided by your emotions than I am. Thus, while all four components of faith are present in each individual, they will vary in their balance and ratio of intensity from person to person.

(3) *The influence of each of these four contributing sources of faith may vary within the life of each individual over a period of years.* For example, when I was a child, my faith was heavily constructed and fortified by tradition. As a teenager, I was keenly sensitive to my intuitive faculties. As a college and seminary student, I was very much guided by my appropriation of reason and intellect. Now, as a mature adult, I feel that I trust my emotional sensitivity more than ever before. Thus, over the course of a lifetime, the force and the contribution of each river ebbs and flows, increases and decreases, dries up to a trickle only to flood forth again.

(4) While each individual may be by nature more attuned to one or two contributive sources of faith, *it is important that there be a healthy balance or ratio between* all *four.* For example, while I was in seminary, I was on a very heavy rational-intellectual "trip." I was constantly being bombarded by lectures, books, new ideas, and stimulating discussions. Being intellectually oriented, I loved it. But there came a time in the midst of my seminary studies when I began to feel spiritually dead. Bothered by this lack of vitality, I went to talk to Dr. Bryant Hicks, a professor whom I highly respected. After

141

listening to my story, Bryant simply said, "You remind me of a bodybuilder I once knew who lifted weights only to develop his shoulders and chest. You have a powerfully built intellectual torso, but it's supported by skinny spiritual legs. It's time you did some spiritual knee bends and spent some time praying and meditating along with your intellectual pursuits. You've allowed your spiritual body to get out of balance."

Dr. Hicks was right. There is a need for all four sources of faith to be deliberately exercised and given free flow into our lives. Faith becomes distorted when one or more rivers are dammed.

(5) *Once the four rivers empty into the lake of faith, it is most difficult to separate their waters.* For, in reality, reason blends quickly into emotion. Intuition and tradition are easily confused. Emotion and intuition can totally merge. So, when we speak of religious faith, we seldom speak of, or are aware of, its component parts. But the four separate rivers continue to flow, making their individual contribution to the end result of faith.

(6) *Finally, it must be emphasized that there is nothing distinctly* Christian *about this fourfold process of faith development.* All that has been said is equally true for the Muslim, the Hindu, the Buddhist, and the animist. For tradition, intuition, reason, and emotion all make their unique contribution to their religious faith as well. The four rivers are universal and flow freely in the lives of all men and women of all faiths and creeds.

20

Five Rivers of Living Water

As I have reflected on the four major rivers that lead to universal religious faith, I have often heard the echo of the voice of Jesus as it is recorded in John 7:38: "He who believes in Me, as Scripture said, 'From his innermost being shall flow rivers of living water.' "

For the Christian, there is a point where river water metaphorically turns into living water—when universal religious faith becomes specifically Christian faith. In this chapter I would like to explore the major contributing factors that lead one to claim the faith of Christianity as his or her own.

THE TESTIMONY OF JESUS

If the four rivers of faith are common to faith development in all religions, what then is unique about the faith of Christianity? There is only one thing. The Christian believes that in a thirty-three-year span of history, God intentionally and forthrightly *revealed himself* in the person of Jesus of Nazareth. In other words, at one point in history, we saw more of God than just a shadow—men and women saw the actual image of God in Jesus Christ. Instead of being a metaphysical concept for philosophers to theorize upon or an intuitive urge for primitive man to sense and respond to, God was suddenly in the midst of history talking and walking and eating with people.

This physical manifestation of God in Jesus is what the writer of 1 John was referring to when he began his letter with the words: "What was from the beginning, what we have heard, what we have seen with our eyes, what we beheld and our hands handled, concerning the Word of Life" (1:1). In other words, God was present among us.

Now, as I write these words and as you read them, all manner of questions immediately pop up, and red lights flash in our intellect. How could Holy God be revealed in a man? How could Jesus be both God and man? Furthermore, how do we know that all of this is any more true than the myths concerning the gods of the ancient Greek pantheon who purportedly would descend from Mount Olympus to live among mortals? What if the story of Jesus is a myth as well—meaningful and profound, yes, but still myth? How can I know all of this is true?

Certainly, these questions and hundreds more are valid and need to be asked. Indeed, it is tempting

144

for me now to get sidetracked and to address these questions within this chapter. But this Christological "question answering" does not lie within the scope of this book. Rather, the point I want to make presently is that once you come face to face with the historical Jesus, you have to decide personally whether or not he was "real." Any historian will tell you that a man named Jesus of Nazareth truly lived. But was he who he claimed to be? Was he right or wrong when he resolutely declared, "He who has seen Me has seen the Father" (John 14:9)?

Sooner or later in the lives of all men and women who contemplate whether or not Christianity is true, there comes a time when the historical evidence must be personally sifted and judged. Christianity is above all a religion rooted in the historical versus the metaphysical. We must ask whether the testimony of the writers of the gospels is true, valid, and historically accurate. We must decide for ourselves whether we really believe that the power of God literally raised Jesus from the dead, thereby proving for all time the authenticity of his life and his message. There comes a time—indeed, many times—to weigh the historical evidence and decide.

There came a time in the lives of the first disciples when they had to weigh the historical and physical evidence and make a decision. It was such an important moment, such a pivotal time, that the Gospels of Matthew, Mark, and Luke all make careful note of it.

It seems that approximately halfway through his

public ministry, Jesus took his disciples aside, and the following conversation ensued (Mark 8:27–29):

> And Jesus went out, along with His disciples, to the villages of Caesarea Philippi; and on the way He questioned His disciples, saying to them, "Who do people say that I am?" And they told Him, saying, "John the Baptist; and others say Elijah; but still others, one of the prophets." And He continued by asking them, "But who do you say that I am?" Peter answered and said to Him, "Thou art the Christ."

Thus, there came a time when the disciples had to decide that Jesus was not just another fiery prophet, a mighty miracle worker, and a profound teacher. Rather, he was the "Christ," the revealer of God.

I'm not sure whether it would have been easier then or now to make that decision. Surely, they had "hands on" evidence. The disciples could see and hear and touch the real thing. But they did not have the comfort—or the excuse—of almost two thousand years of Christian tradition to fall back upon, to encourage them, to coax them into agreement.

But, it really doesn't matter whether deciding about Christ was easy or hard for the disciples. They still had to weigh the facts as they understood them and to make a decision. And so do we.

As was seen in the first section of this book, my decision came as a twenty-two-year-old who had just completed a double college major in religion and psychology. I was acquainted with "the facts." I had read the books, asked the questions, heard the myriad answers, plodded through diverse theologies. But sitting on a stone wall late one night in the mountains of North Carolina, I still had to make a decision. I still had to answer the question, "But who do *you* say that I am?"

The point is this. Christianity is a *historical* religion. Christian faith—not "religious" faith—must be rooted in the events of history. And we must be our own historical critics.

Thus, in addition to the universal contributing rivers of tradition, intuition, reason, and emotion that affect the faith development of *all* religions, we must also add the unique Christian criterion for faith—historical evidence. In a moment of time, was God revealed in Jesus Christ? You must make that decision. And your decision will greatly affect the development of your religious faith.

THE SPIRIT OF GOD

In addition to the uniquely Christian concept of God's being revealed in the historical event of Jesus Christ, Christians have also believed that there is yet another major influence on the development of Christian faith. That influence is the ministry of the Holy Spirit. Quite apart from intuition or emotion—as well as in cooperation with them—the traditional Christian perspective is that the Spirit of God works within the perceptions of men and women to bring them to a deeper and more mature faith in God.

As we read the New Testament, particularly Acts, the Gospel of John, and the epistles of Paul, it is very clear that the earliest Christians firmly believed that it was the Holy Spirit of God who played the most dominant role in bringing people to believe that God was revealed in Jesus Christ. More than the historical events of Jesus and the apostolic eye-witness to that event, it was the Holy Spirit that persuaded people to accept the *kerygma*—the early church's proclamation about Jesus.

As we read the Gospel of John, we find that the Holy Spirit is depicted as serving five functions in its persuasive role—those of:

- witness (15:26),
- teacher (14:26),
- judge (16:7–11),
- guide (16:13–15), and
- helper (14:16–18).

Serving in these diverse capacities, the Holy Spirit was a major influence—perhaps *the* major influence—in the earliest Christian's faith development.

Very quickly, however, the dominant role of the Holy Spirit in the life of the New Testament church began to wane. Addressing this fact, Dr. Henlee Barnette, Senior Professor of Christian Ethics at Southern Baptist Theological Seminary, states,

The early church was Spirit-centered. Its ethic was an ethic of the Holy Spirit. As time passed, the Spirit became peripheral and secondary in the life of the church. Toward the end of the first century, the Logos doctrine tended to supplant the Spirit as the life force of the churches. By the time of the Middle

148

Ages the Logos had become a metaphysical principle rather than a living personal Lord whose work was made effective by the Spirit. Today, organized effort, rather than the power of the Spirit, has tended to become the pattern of the church. The Spirit has been retained as a doctrine without being effective in Christian experience.[1]

Agreeing with Barnette, Stanley Hopper writes,

The doctrine of the Holy Spirit is at once the most central and most neglected doctrine of the Christian faith. It is the most central in the sense that everything in the Gospels is energized and motivated through its agency. . . . Yet, the doctrine has remained peripheral for the most part in the long history of doctrinal thinking.[2]

Whether or not the contemporary Christian church does—or should—put enough emphasis and acknowledgment on the workings of the Holy Spirit is a point that will not be argued here. It has been my experience, however, and it is my testimony, that the Holy Spirit is a very potent contributor to the development of faith.

As I look back upon the continuing evolution of my faith, I can see moments when I know I was influenced by far more than reason, intuition, emotion, tradition, or my own convictions concerning the historical testimony of Jesus. For instance, there was the night that I stood alone looking out a college dormitory window, torn by a civil war within me over whether to continue my academic—and very threatening—studies of Christianity. I am now convinced it was the Holy Spirit who was the most persuasive factor in my decision to go back to the classroom. (This influence of the Holy Spirit was what I was referring to when I wrote, in the first half of this book, "Sometimes in life we are pushed. At other times we are drawn. On that night, I was drawn forward by what I can only call the gentle grace of God.") I am equally convinced that four years later, as I sat on that stone wall in North Carolina, it was the influence of the Holy Spirit that enabled me to "bet my life that Christ is right."

Now, I must confess that there have been moments in my life when I have desperately wanted to feel the presence of the Holy Spirit and have felt absolutely nothing—moments when there has been only a hollow, aching void. But there have been enough times when I have been convinced of the power and the presence of the Holy Spirit to enable me to know that the Spirit's influence on my faith development—and your faith development—is real. And even in those moments of experiencing the void, the obvious, aching absence of the Spirit has been enough to convince me of its reality.

Thus, within the testimony of the New Testament, within my own testimony, and within the testimony of thousands of other Christians, there is a loud and continuous voice affirming that the Holy Spirit of God is also a dominant factor and influence in the development of religious—and in particular, Christian—faith.

150

THE TEACHABLE MOMENT

As a graduate student engaged in research in the area of adult development, I discovered a technical term called the "teachable moment," which has come to have not only an educational, but also a theological, meaning for me. The concept has been popularized by Dr. Robert J. Havighurst, a professor of adult education at North Carolina State University. Havighurst defines the "teachable moment" in the following manner:

There are sensitive periods or critical periods when a human being is especially able to learn quickly through certain types of experiences. . . . Efforts at teaching which would have been largely wasted if they had come earlier, give gratifying results when they come at the teachable moment, when the task should be learned.[3]

In essence, the teachable moment is that time in life when events converge that make us want to learn—indeed, enable us to learn—certain things we were unwilling or incapable of learning previously.

Recently, I built a five-foot fence for my golden retriever, Beau. Prior to building the fence, I had tried to no avail to teach Beau to jump over a two-foot hurdle for field trials. Beau was hopeless. He was landlocked. However, when the next-door neighbor's female dog came into season, it was amazing how quickly and almost effortlessly Beau learned

151

to leap over that five-foot fence! The teachable moment had arrived.

Now, what does the teachable moment have to do with the development of Christian faith? A lot! Recently, I was reading *The Seven Story Mountain*, the autobiography of Thomas Merton, the great twentieth-century mystic and spiritual giant. In this book, Merton relates how he had never been religiously inclined as a youth, adolescent, or young adult. But then certain events transpired in his life that forced him to seek spiritual truth. During this time of searching, he reached a teachable moment in regard to religious faith. Merton described his receptivity to learning in this way:

> But now I had been beaten into the semblance of some kind of humility by misery and confusion and perplexity and secret, interior fear, my ploughed soul was better ground for the reception of good seed.[4]

In a sense, the teachable moment comes when our fields are plowed, when the hard dirt is turned up and the soft soil exposed, and when we are vulnerable and receptive to new knowledge and perspectives pertaining to Christianity.

Perhaps my own most teachable spiritual moment came during that traumatic Christmas season when I experienced, for the first time in my life, an anxiety attack and resultant depression. Always before, my approach to God and to faith had been very cerebral. But suddenly, nothing made sense in my life anymore. I was forced to deal with new emotions and suddenly was willing to experience God in new ways. I learned much about "death and resurrection theology" that would have been nonsensical had I not had this experience. The paradoxes of Christian faith became clearer to me.

Let me hasten to say, however, that teachable moments are not always brought on by negative or painful experiences. Many times, I have seen people deeply affected in their faith by the birth of a child, a beautiful sunset, an unexpected present given "for no good reason," or even the viewing of a profound movie. All these things and hundreds more "plow our fields" and make us teachable.

So the convergence of external situations which results in teachable moments has much to do with faith development. Without these moments of receptivity, faith might never grow nor mature.

THE FELLOWSHIP OF FAITH

In the course of my life, I have come to take Jesus very seriously when he said, "For where two or three are gathered together in My name, there I am in their midst" (Matt. 18:20). I have found that intimate friendship, work, play, relaxation, worship—in short, being in community—with other Christians has within it a catalytic agent for the development of faith. It seems that when two or more Christians share their thoughts, their joys, their sorrows, their doubts, and all the other things that compose life, once again the basic "bread and fish" substance of faith is multiplied instead of consumed. It has been my experience that Christian faith grows when it is nurtured on the food of fellowship.

Now, I firmly believe that the type of fellowship of which I speak is fundamentally different from the intentional propagation of religious tradition. I have been in churches that greatly stressed tradition, mouthed the creeds, sang the great hymns, and spoke in King James English—and yet did little to help my faith grow. And I have experienced Bible studies in my living room, bull sessions while fishing, and after-church coffees around someone's kitchen table that somehow bolstered my faith in an uncontrived and unexpected way. This is not to say I have not experienced the same in formal worship or within the life of the institutional church. I have. But I am saying that the fellowship of which I speak has nothing to do with traditions nor institutions. It has everything to do with spiritual interpersonal intimacy.

There is a quotation by the famous Swiss physician-theologian, Paul Tournier, that has become one of the central mottoes in the living of my life. In his book, *The Meaning of Persons,* Tournier states,

> We become fully conscious only of what we are able to express to someone else. We may already have had a certain inner intuition about it, but it must remain vague so long as it is unformulated.[5]

This statement first developed great meaning for me within a psychotherapeutic context. Through my

154

own experience in counseling, I came to understand Tournier as saying we cannot undo our own interpersonal problems, complexes, and neuroses by ourselves. We must be able to verbalize and emotionally express our conflicts to a trusted friend, counselor, or therapist before the knots within us can become untied. Not to verbalize our conflicts is like trying to untie a twisted and tightly knotted rope with only one hand. Unknotting a psyche requires two hands, two minds, two perspectives, and two people growing together.

Recently, however, I have come to see that Tournier's statement applies not only to the psychological, but to the spiritual realm as well. It is infinitely difficult to mature in our faith development by ourselves. As in the psychotherapeutic process, we must be able to express in some way—including communal silence—our doubts and our convictions, our fears and our courage, our praises and our sorrows, our losses and our thanksgiving. It is only when this is done—where "two or more are gathered in My name"—that the rope binding the door of faith is loosened a little more.

I believe that Jesus was well aware of the importance of fellowship for faith development. It was for this reason that one of the first things he did in his ministry was to surround himself with a community of twelve other followers. Not only did Jesus teach his disciples, but he shared openly with them his own struggles and victories. Bruce Larson first called my attention to this fact in his book, *Ask Me to Dance.* He wrote:

During his three years of ministry Jesus must have been a very open person. How else could we know about his temptation in the wilderness? No other human being was there. How could we know about his discouragements, his sorrows, his fear of the cross, his agony before God as he wrestled with the Father's will? We know about them only because our Lord disclosed them to faithful men who passed them on to us.[6]

Thus, even Jesus, the Image of God, needed fellowship with other seekers in order for his own faith to be nurtured.

As I think back upon my life, I remember moments gathered with my family around the fireplace, inhaling the cigarette smoke of the Marlboro Crew, packed with my Grain family in the close quarters of the Grain Wagon, pouring my heart out in Stan Nelson's office, holding my wife's and sons' hands while praying at the dinner table. And when I think of these moments of intimate fellowship, faith comes alive. It is a faith that firmly comprehends and affirms that ultimately nothing can separate us from the love of God, the love of each other, and the love of life. Within the bond of fellowship, we are inspired to have faith in the eternal unity of life.

THE PROCESS OF FOLLOWING

I have reserved for last the one stimulus to the development of faith that perhaps means most to me at the present moment. This final contributor is simply the action-commitment of "following."

It is interesting that when Jesus walked down the shoreline of the lives of his first disciples, he did not ask them to *believe* in him or to consent to a creed or even to adhere to a philosophy of life. He simply said, "Follow me."

The older I get and the longer I profess to be a Christian disciple, the more significant the concept of following becomes to me. More than anything else, it means that faith is more of a *process* than an *event.* Now what do I mean by this?

From one perspective, this book has been a reporting of *events* in my life. Discovering there was no Santa Claus was an event. It happened in a specific place, at a specific time, when I was a specific age. Likewise, my decision to "bet my life that Christ was right," my experience of resurrection in the Atlanta graveyard, and my decision to attend seminary were all *events* of faith. But as I look backward over the scope of my life, the singular events merge and become instead one continuous *process.* And that process is what I call "following."

From my present perspective, what I rationally believe about Christianity is not as important to me as that I continue to follow. My beliefs concerning a lot of theological concepts may be wrong. Or they may be right. But either way, what I believe will not ultimately be as important as that I persistently and doggedly attempt to follow Christ to the best of my understanding. Once again, allow me to quote my never-met friend, Leslie Weatherhead:

If Christ can—and He does—hold in utter loyalty the hearts of St. Francis and John Knox, of Calvin and St. Theresa, of General Booth and Pope John, of Billy Graham and Albert Schweitzer, who hold irreconcilably different beliefs about Him, how can belief and uniformity of belief be vitally important?[7]

I believe that it was to this exact line of reasoning that Professor Herbert Butterfield, a venerated chancellor of Cambridge University, was addressing himself when he repeatedly and somewhat emphatically told his students, "Hold to Christ, and for the rest be totally uncommitted."[8] In essence, belief is not the ultimate test of Christian faith. Rather, the test is whether or not we continue to follow, continue the process, continue the faith.

Thirty years from now, I may reread sections from this book and shake my head and say, "Scott, you were wrong." Over the years my belief structure may change. But I hope my resolve to follow will stay strong.

Ultimately, this experience of following is what Albert Schweitzer was referring to when he wrote:

He will reveal Himself through the toils, the conflicts, the sufferings which they shall pass through in His fellowship, and, as an ineffable mystery, they shall learn in their own experience Who He is.[9]

It is our own experience of following him that results in the "ineffable mystery" of faith development. Yes, faith is developed by reason, intuition,

158

tradition, and emotion. Faith is spawned through reflection on the historical Jesus and interaction with the Holy Spirit. Faith is prompted through the catalysts of the teachable moment and the intimacy of fellowship. But when all is said and done—when events flow together into a process—faith is ultimately developed by following.

And so, continue the river's course. Do not be afraid to think your greatest thoughts, feel your deepest emotions, and intuit the subtle truths of the universe. And when temporality merges into eternity, may your epitaph of faith simply be, "I followed."

Synopsis

Within the pages of this book, I have presented the belief that the development of individual religious faith must always be seen against the backdrop of biography. How we have lived and what we have experienced are the brushes that paint the picture of faith upon the canvas of our lives. Theology cannot be divorced from biography.

As I have analyzed the story of my life and have reflected upon the lives of others, I have become convinced that nine elements are instrumental in the formulation of religious—and in particular, Christian—faith. I list them here as a summary and concluding statement:

- the inheritance of tradition
- the perception of intuition
- the insight of reason
- the experience of emotion
- the testimony of Jesus
- the influence of the Holy Spirit
- the impact of the teachable moment
- the catalyst of fellowship
- the process of following

Notes

To the Reader

1. Penrose St. Amant, "Communicating the Gospel in the Eighties," *The Quarterly Review* (April 1981): 68.

Chapter 4

1. Leslie D. Weatherhead, *The Christian Agnostic* (Nashville: Abingdon, 1965), 87.

Chapter 10

1. D. Elton Trueblood, *A Place to Stand* (New York: Harper & Row, 1969), 60.

Chapter 17

1. Albert Schweitzer, *The Quest of the Historical Jesus* (New York: Macmillan, 1969), 403.

Chapter 19

1. George Gallup, Jr., and David Poling, *The Search for America's Faith* (Nashville: Abingdon, 1965), 155.
2. Weatherhead, *The Christian Agnostic*, 71.
3. Emil Brunner, *The Christian Doctrine of God*, vol. 1 (Philadelphia: Westminster, 1950), 117.
4. Ibid., 117.
5. Trueblood, *A Place to Stand*, 24.
6. James S. Stewart, *King For Ever* (Nashville: Abingdon, 1975), 25.

163

CHAPTER 20

1. Henlee Barnette, *Introducing Christian Ethics* (Nashville: Broadman, 1961), 93.

2. Stanley R. Hopper, "Holy Spirit," in *A Handbook of Christian Theology,* ed. Marvin Halverson and Arthur A. Cohen (New York: World, 1958), 170.

3. Robert J. Havighurst, *Developmental Tasks and Education,* 3rd ed. (New York: David McKay, 1974), 6–7.

4. Thomas Merton, *The Seven Story Mountain* (Garden City, NY: Image, 1948), 256.

5. Paul Tournier, *The Meaning of Persons* (New York: Harper & Row, 1971), 17.

6. Bruce Larson, *Ask Me to Dance* (Waco: Word, 1972), 44.

7. Weatherhead, *The Christian Agnostic,* 71.

8. Herbert Butterfield, *Christianity and History* (New York: Scribner's, 1950), 146.

9. Schweitzer, *The Quest of the Historical Jesus,* 403.